Law and Mineral Wealth

Law
and Mineral Wealth

The Legal Profile of the Wisconsin Mining Industry

JAMES A. LAKE

The University of Wisconsin Press

Madison, 1962

Published by
THE UNIVERSITY OF WISCONSIN PRESS
430 Sterling Court, Madison 6, Wisconsin

Copyright © 1962 by the Regents of the University of Wisconsin

Printed in the United States of America by
Vail-Ballou Press, Inc., Binghamton, New York

Library of Congress Catalog Card Number 62–9261

Preface

THIS IS A story about an industry and about law and about the relation between the two. The industry is mining in the state of Wisconsin; the law is mainly that embodied in the statutes and judge-made law of Wisconsin, though some federal laws also enter the picture. The span of the story is roughly one hundred years, from mid-nineteenth century to mid-twentieth. The purpose is to examine how law influenced development of the mineral resources of the state and how this economic effort affected legal order.

The discussion avoids technical legal doctrine. This is not a handbook to help a lawyer brief a case. Thus, I have often translated legal terms into layman's words, though some of the ideas shaped in legal concepts defy this treatment.

The book examines the subject matter with prime emphasis upon the time dimension: it is a study in legal history. It attempts to respond to complaints such as Professor William Baskerville Hamilton made when he observed that "the legal profession in this country evinces such an unwillingness to write legal history that the historians will have to begin upon the painful education that will enable them to fill the vacuum" (*Anglo-American Law on the Frontier* [Durham, N.C., 1953], p. ix).

Law is a product of men's efforts—and of their failings. Especially within the frame of values developed in the growth of the United States, law has formed an important part of general history. Over a century ago, De Tocqueville observed that the nature of the United States Constitution turned almost every political question into a judicial question. Had he traveled the United States in 1950, De Tocqueville would have noted the same feature in the handling of many economic and social problems. Justice Felix Frankfurter has characterized Supreme Court opinions as a "good mirror" of our civilization but, as he also pointed out, a mirror of which historians have "little availed themselves" ("Chief Justices I Have Known," *Virginia Law Review,* XXXIX [1953], 894–95). Of like relevance to our general history, and as little used, are the records of state trial and appellate courts, state legislatures, boards of county supervisors, administrative bodies, and other agencies of legal order.

This book presents the main aspects of the legal history of one industry in one state. I hope that it may be a building block in the structure of larger legal studies which someday will grow into the legal history of the United States.

J. A. L.

Lincoln, Nebraska
July, 1961

Contents

Law and Mineral Wealth

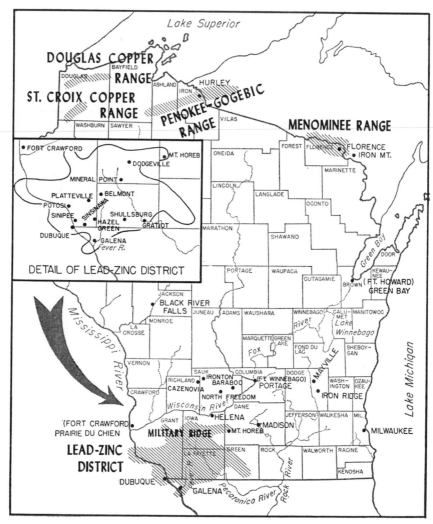

Map of Wisconsin showing mining areas

1

The Setting

GEOGRAPHY AND GEOLOGY, the course of immigration, the development of markets and transport, the progress of science and technology, the ups and downs of finance and speculation—all contributed to the setting of facts and forces within which developed the legal history of the exploitation of Wisconsin's mineral wealth. In this, as in most areas of social affairs, the law's role was limited but nonetheless important, since it dealt in critical respects with the relationships among these diverse factors. In this broad sense the social history of law deals with "order"—with the ordering of relations. Thus, it is essential to the kind of history this book tells that we begin by sketching the nature of the principal elements—both the relatively constant facts of nature and the dynamic processes of social institutions—whose patterning determined the problems brought to law in this field.

This first chapter describes the physical facts and economic institutions within which the legal order developed. It is a short nonlegal history of the mineral industry of Wisconsin arranged by types of mineral wealth, starting first with lead, then zinc, copper, and iron in that order. This order roughly corresponds with the chronological order in which the minerals became important in the state's economy.

The trans-Allegheny region possessed two areas with lead ore in commercial quantities. One existed in Missouri and the other largely

in Wisconsin. Both of these areas bordered on good water routes—
including the greatest of all, the Mississippi—and were thus favorably situated for development in the prerailroad era. The Wisconsin
deposits, known as the upper Mississippi deposits, were located in
the extreme southwestern corner of the state and in adjoining
areas of Illinois on the south and Iowa on the southwest.[1] Within
the state of Wisconsin, the counties of Grant, Iowa, and Lafayette
contained the bulk of the lead deposits. These three counties, located
just beyond the reach of the great glaciers of the ice age, escaped
the leveling action of the ice sheets and consequently possessed
rugged terrain featured by deep ravines, steep slopes, and fast streams
with deep courses.

The region's most pronounced topographical feature was the "military ridge." Running from Mt. Horeb west to meet the Mississippi
just south of the mouth of the Wisconsin River, this elongated hump
of elevated ground divided the lead region into a northern and a
southern watershed. Streams running northward from the ridge's
crest drained into the Wisconsin River; streams descending south-
ward flowed into the Rock and Mississippi rivers. The military road
built in 1835 from Green Bay to Prairie du Chien followed the crest
of the ridge, and a few years later a territorial road from Milwaukee
to the lead district followed a similar route. In 1881 the Chicago and
Northwestern Railway Company located its roadbed upon the ridge.
By using the crest of the ridge all these roads avoided the engineering difficulties of bridging the rugged ravines and streams located
at lower elevations.

A vertical section of a representative tract in Wisconsin's lead
region would first show seven to ten feet of topsoil fertile enough
to grow such crops as wheat, hay, and corn. Formed by the im-
perceptible action of oxidation, hydration, temperature changes, and
plant and animal action upon the underlying rock strata, this topsoil made the region valuable for horticultural pursuits. When
miners deserted the lead deposits much of the populace shifted to
farming, and the region suffered no great population decline nor
much economic harm. Shallow holes dug here and there by wander-

ing miners did not permanently damage the utility of the land for agriculture.

The second horizontal layer, 125 to 250 feet thick, was the most important. This was the Galena dolomite, which contained the greatest number of lead deposits. The third layer, 40 to 125 feet of Platteville or Trenton limestone, contained a few lead deposits but not nearly as many as the Galena dolomite. Beneath the third layer was the St. Peter sandstone, 70 to 100 feet thick, and then the lower magnesian limestone, 40 to 250 feet thick.

Early miners extracted most of their lead ore from the rock strata immediately beneath the topsoil. Veins of lead ore in the Galena dolomite pitched downward at an angle, but usually stopped, or "pinched out" as the miners put it, at the St. Peter sandstone. For many years miners speculated about what was beneath the sandstone, but their demands that the state finance the cost of deep shafts which would end the uncertainty were disregarded.

Before white miners arrived in Wisconsin in the 1820's, sovereignty over the lead area passed from France to Great Britain in 1763 and finally to the United States in 1783. Throughout the entire period of French and British control and for several decades of United States sovereignty, various Indian tribes—Chippewa, Potawatomi, Sauk, Fox, Menominee, and Winnebago—roamed the lead area, claiming it either as their homeland or as their hunting grounds. Before 1820 white inhabitants were largely limited to the fur traders and missionaries and to the military personnel who manned a line of forts extending from Fort Howard at Green Bay to Fort Winnebago at the portage between the Wisconsin and Fox rivers, and on to Fort Crawford at Prairie du Chien. With one exception, the economy of the area, Indian and white, centered upon the fur trade. As early as 1788 Julien Dubuque obtained a valuable prerogative to mine and smelt lead ore on the western bank of the Mississippi near the present city of Dubuque, Iowa. With shrewdness, he gained the confidence of many Indians and employed them to work his claim. Besides Dubuque only a few Indian miners tapped the wealth of the lead area. The Indians gathered surface ore and smelted it by heaping ore upon a pile of logs, firing the logs, and gathering the purified residue after the fire and heat subsided.[2]

As early as 1816 mining activity had begun around Galena, on the Fever River in Illinois, although the productivity of the Missouri mines still held major interest. By 1822 many optimistic reports of the riches of the Wisconsin and Illinois area had filtered down to the Missouri miners, and large-scale operations, gauged by 1820 standards, were underway on the Fever River. By 1827 a real mining boom in Illinois was evident.[3] In April or May of 1828 lead was found at Mineral Point, Wisconsin, and within a few years miners explored all of the area between the Fever River on the south, and the Wisconsin River on the north.[4]

Wisconsin's first miners were men of the frontier or men who readily adapted to frontier conditions. They were rough, tough, ingenious improvisers. Fisticuffs, profanity, drinking, card playing, gambling, and even dueling were commonplace activities with which the legal order had to contend. Many Wisconsin miners had migrated northward from the Missouri mines. They came prepared to use the knowledge and tricks of the trade learned there. The accepted method of locating ore was unscientific—a hit-or-miss search. Many prospectors depended upon their ability to recognize surface indications of ore. Practical knowledge was indispensable. Some Missouri miners had been moderately successful; these brought their savings to Wisconsin.

Lead settled southwestern Wisconsin. The ore attracted men mostly from areas south of Wisconsin—from Kentucky, Ohio, Illinois, and Missouri. Few Yankees from New York and the New England states came to the upper Mississippi lead region, and the percentage of foreign-born inhabitants was smaller than in any other area of the state. The rule of native-born inhabitants was broken in one respect. A large contingent of Cornish miners arrived in the early 1830's from the depleted mines of Cornwall.[5] These resourceful men generally worked mines abandoned by others. Employing skills learned at home, the Cornish recovered many pounds of lead ore, often from far beneath the surface and from flooded areas. From the beginning, the lead area possessed a population which distinguished it from the eastern lakefront area of the state where Yankee agriculturalists predominated.

The single economy and common southern birthplace of most of the lead area's inhabitants were conducive to development of a strong political power bloc. For many years the lead area dominated the politics of the territory and state. Except for a period of a little over three years, an avowed protagonist of the region's interest, Colonel Henry Dodge, was governor of the territory during the twelve years of its existence. After statehood in 1848, the lead area supplied the first state governor, Nelson Dewey of Grant County. At the close of Dewey's term the area's political influence decreased, and thereafter its political leaders were required to effect compromises to secure legislation.[6]

The bulky and weighty character of lead presented transportation problems of large proportions. Before the development of rail transportation two water routes moved Wisconsin lead to eastern markets. Lead from Mineral Point, Dodgeville, and other Wisconsin settlements floated down the Pecatonica and Rock rivers to the Mississippi, to New Orleans, and into the gulf on the journey to the eastern seaboard. Galena, Illinois, became the dominant marshalling and supply center at the western terminus of this route. Wisconsin miners became extremely jealous of the Galena dominance and particularly annoyed by the profiteering of Galena merchants and their refusal to accept lead-area bank notes at par. To compete with Galena, Wisconsin miners sought to locate a new Wisconsin town, Sinipee, on the Mississippi, but efforts failed when sickness made the location uninhabitable. Unsuccessful endeavors to improve Mississippi River navigation at Potosi, Wisconsin, by constructing a canal to bypass rapids were spurred on by the desire to destroy the supreme position of Galena.

The second transportation route employed the Wisconsin and Fox rivers to gain entrance to the Great Lakes system, which, together with the Erie Canal, carried lead to eastern markets. This route was faster and cheaper than the Mississippi route. By 1837 river steamers were ascending the Wisconsin River as far as Fort Winnebago at Portage. A tower to manufacture shot was constructed at Helena in Iowa County on a bluff overlooking the Wisconsin River, and it operated until 1861. Manufacturing at the tower suffered during the 1857 panic and upon the failure of the rail line to the Mississippi to pass close enough to the tower to be beneficial.

Competing overland transportation quickly developed. By 1836 six, eight, or more yoke of oxen plodding eastward pulling wagons heavily loaded with the output of Wisconsin's lead mines were a common sight. The same wagons carried agricultural products from eastern Wisconsin westward, and southeastern and southwestern Wisconsin joined forces to battle for better roads. Rail lines appeared around the mid-century, linking the two areas, but by that time peak lead production had passed.

The history of economic activity in the lead region may be divided into two periods with 1848 as the dividing line. Prior to that year lead production expanded year by year, and the growth was remarkably rapid for that time. It has been said: "There are few people except the old pioneer residents perhaps, who have even the remotest idea of the vast quantities of lead ore that has been taken from the lead mines. Nor is it possible to gain any correct statistics of the amount." [7]

Steady development and constantly increasing production figures were the rule until 1848. In that year and the years immediately following, many Wisconsin miners deserted their lead diggings for California gold fields. No one accurately tabulated the extent of the migration, but perhaps one-half of the miners succumbed to the lure of gold. [8]

Far western gold was not the sole motivation for the migration. By 1848 mining in the lead region had become difficult and expensive. Easily secured surface deposits were exhausted; deeper shafts and drainage works were necessary. By 1848 most lead-bearing acres were privately owned. Miners who owned no land or lacked capital to buy it, or who detested the hard work of deep mining were easily enticed westward.

The second stage, from 1848 to mid-twentieth century, saw several spurts of lead-mining activity, but for the most part the period was characterized by relatively stable production figures. Between 1911 and 1931 lead production reached above 3,000 short tons per year only in 1911, 1912, 1916, 1918, 1919, and 1920. During that same time span, zinc production, tonnage-wise, exceeded that of lead in every year.

After the Civil War the importance of lead mining in the state's economy declined, while that of zinc increased. This pronounced shift prompted state geologist Chamberlin to announce about 1878 that the lead district should thereafter be called the zinc region.

Chronologically, zinc was the second mineral to draw the attention of miners. It was quite often found in the same rock strata as lead and often mixed with it. During the early history of the state, lack of knowledge about smelting zinc made it useless to the miners and large quantities were mined but discarded. Some zinc ore was even used to build roads. When zinc-smelting methods were later perfected, this zinc ore was recovered.

As early as 1842 zinc ore was identified. A publication at that time prophesied that in the future zinc would "become an object of importance."[9] Eighteen years later one form of zinc ore found in Wisconsin, known as "drybone," was smelted successfully. By the close of the Civil War scientific knowledge made usable the higher grade zinc found in the state, "blackjack."

Efforts to found a zinc-smelting industry in Wisconsin failed. By 1859 drybone was smelted at Mineral Point. In 1864 eastern capitalists spent $100,000 to erect large-scale works there, but the venture ultimately collapsed.[10] Lack of coal or some other cheap fuel supply was an insurmountable obstacle. Over the years most of Wisconsin's zinc ore was transported outside the state for processing.

At the mid-twentieth-century point, additional geological explorations had pinpointed quite large lead and zinc reserves. Zinc reserves then exceeded lead manyfold. Future mining, it appeared, would depend upon world market conditions and federal tariff policy, which by that time together largely dictated the price for domestic lead and zinc, and hence, indirectly, the scale of production. In 1942 20 zinc mines were operating: 4 in Grant County, 3 in Iowa County, and 13 in Lafayette County.

The history of iron mining in Wisconsin rivals in glamour and interest the story of lead. The state of Wisconsin was created between two of the greatest iron-mining regions in the United States. On the west, Minnesota possessed the greatest of all United States deposits—the Mesabi range—and boasted other iron ore areas—the Cuyuna and the Vermillion ranges. To the east in Michigan's Upper Peninsula lay the Marquette, Gogebic, and Menominee ranges. Though the Gogebic and Menominee ranges extended across the Michigan-Wisconsin boundary, Wisconsin's high-grade iron ore resources could compare with neither of its neighboring states. Its low-grade iron ore potential was large, however.

The Baraboo district was the first explored. This district extended for twenty-eight miles in an east-west direction across Sauk and Columbia counties, varying in width from two to twelve miles. Some iron was mined at Ironton in Sauk County during the Civil War. However, the activity was small. The total annual production of all mines in the state during the early part of that decade never amounted to more than 7,500 tons.

Many persons, including geologists, published general, optimistic statements concerning large iron-ore deposits north of the Wisconsin River, but no report ever pinpointed the areas with accuracy. In 1873 the Northwestern Iron Company constructed a furnace at Cazenovia in Richland County, about six miles southwest of Ironton. Even before the plant was completed, it was moved to Fruitport, Michigan. In 1887 the Douglas Iron Mining Company explored extensively on the Baraboo range in Sauk County, when diggings from a farm well showed cherts containing iron ore. Forty thousand dollars were spent to sink shafts and some high-grade ore was discovered. The property was mined from 1889 to 1899 by the Chicago and Northwestern Railway Company. It then passed into the hands of W. G. La Rue, Robert B. Whiteside, and Herman Grotophorst. In April of 1900 this group discovered additional ore at a site close to North Freedom in Sauk County. The great depth of the deposits and the presence of water increased production costs so much that operations were suspended. By 1914 there was no activity on the Baraboo range.

Black River Falls, lying about eighty miles northwest of Baraboo, also early aspired to become the center of a huge iron-mining district. On August 14, 1856, the *Black River Falls Banner* reported: "The iron ore within the area of forty acres square will prove inexhaustible for centuries to come, and it is of the best quality." An iron-mining company, the Black River Falls Iron Company, was formed by G. M. Wetzel, Charles Hauser, Theobald Metzger, Augustus Wierich, and John Lewis, but the promoters soon gave up. All returned to their native Germany but Lewis, who shifted his interests to lumbering.

The lack of success of high-grade iron ore mining in the Black River Falls area did not alter the fact that the surrounding area was rich in low-grade iron ore deposits. In 1945 experts estimated that Jackson County deposits could produce 300,000 tons of iron concentrates annually for the next forty years. In 1945 renewed interest in the area was evident when Inland Steel Company acquired mineral rights to 3,000 acres. Without startling new technological discoveries or direct or indirect subsidies from local, state, or federal government the low-grade ore deposits could not compete with high-grade sources.

The major area of pre-Civil War iron mining was on the Iron Ridge in Dodge County. In 1848 a crude blast furnace was constructed there. In 1854 the Northwestern Iron Company was formed to operate a smelter in the area. Minor Civil War activity was succeeded by increased action. By 1870 nine-tenths of the state's total iron ore output was from Dodge County. The "hard" Iron Ridge ores found a ready market at Cleveland, Chicago, St. Louis, and Wyandotte where they were mixed with the "softer" Lake Superior ores.

The Northwestern Iron Company remained in business under the same family ownership until 1908. After it was sold in that year, it continued to operate. On the eve of World War I it produced around 175,000 tons of pig iron each year. From 1892 to 1928 Dodge County deposits produced 2,380,000 tons of ore.

Post-Civil War activity concentrated on iron deposits in two areas of northern Wisconsin. The first was the Menominee range of Michigan, which extended westward across the boundary line into Florence County, Wisconsin. About 1873 Nelson Powell Hulst developed properties on the Michigan side of the line. Soon thereafter the Chicago and Northwestern built a rail line into Wisconsin. Deposits in Florence County were opened and ore was shipped to Escanaba, Michigan, and then by water to smelters. Florence County mines produced 7,250,000 tons of ore between 1881 and 1932. The 1930 depression severely injured Florence County iron mining; estimates then placed almost one-half of the county's population on relief. After 1932 little iron mining was evident in the county.

The second northern Wisconsin iron deposits consisted of a westward extension of the Gogebic range of Michigan, an extension commonly called the Penokee range. Although this range extended fifty-two miles across the counties of Iron, Ashland, and Bayfield, the eastern-most thirteen miles of the range around Hurley, Wisconsin, were most fully developed.

Interest in the Penokee range antedated actual development by many years. As early as 1858 a mining company, the Wisconsin and Lake Superior Mining Company, requested I. A. Lapham to survey the range. Accompanied by Edward Daniels of the State Geological Survey, Lapham surveyed a portion of the range and reported magnetic ore, grading 78 to 89 per cent iron. Nothing other than a favorable stockholders' report resulted from this investigation.

Captain Nat. D. Moore "discovered" iron on the Penokee range in 1872 when he noted hematite around roots of a tree which had been felled by a windstorm. Moore formed the Iron Chief Mining Company and acquired almost all of the range property on the Wisconsin side of the Montreal River. In 1884, 1,000 tons of ore were shipped from the range to Cleveland.

In 1885 the greatest mining boom in the history of the state hit

Wisconsin. Hurley grew by leaps and bounds from a gathering of log huts to a town with brick stores. The Hurley newspaper, the *Iron Tribune,* reporting "facts" to its readers, "conservatively" valued the range at $23,465,000. Mines rapidly increased in value, often from 100 to 1,200 per cent.

John E. Burton and two associates purchased the Aurora mine. Using knowledge he had gained in promoting the Tilden silver mines in Colorado, Burton soon increased the value of Aurora stock 500 per cent. Before the 1886 season opened Burton controlled eight mines. He constructed one of the finest hotels in the midwest at Hurley. Governor "Uncle Jerry" Rusk presided at the opening and almost every state dignitary from Lieutenant Governor Fifield down attended. Burton's wealth was estimated at $1,410,000 and Moore's as even greater. Moore invested some of his wealth in a gaudy vest garnished with black onyx buttons set with diamonds. At the zenith of the boom the Penokee range boasted twenty-two companies with a nominal capital stock of $40,000,000.

The beginning of the end occurred in late 1887 when many people found it increasingly difficult to dispose of the gilt-edged, high-priced stock they had purchased. It was not long until no market for Penokee stocks existed at all. Burton and Moore, black onyx buttons and all, were carried under.

Throughout the boom and in spite of its wasteful aspects, ore was mined and marketed from many places on the Penokee range. In 1885 the Aurora mine shipped 5,256 tons, and production increased to 100,000 tons the next year. The Colby mine shipped 300,000 tons prior to the close of the 1886 season.

By August 1945 the Cary mine and the Montreal mine, both near Hurley, were the only mines producing. From its opening in 1886 to 1945 the Cary shipped a total of 9,000,000 tons of ore. In 1944 its management spent $2,000,000 in improvements. The Montreal produced 27,000,000 tons of ore from 1886 to 1945. High production costs characterized both mines. The great depth of the deposits was responsible: the Montreal operated 2,800 feet below the surface.

Although some non-metallic mineral resources contributed more to the economy and development of the state through the years than lead, zinc, or iron, they were often overlooked when men estimated Wisconsin's natural wealth. Such resources as building stone, crushed stone, sand, gravel, clay, limestone, and marble seldom received special attention from the legislature, the judiciary, or the executive. The abundance of these resources and the fact that no one besides geologists thought of them as mineral wealth, accounted for the lack of their distinctive treatment by the legal order. Many of these resources were subject to the same laws that were applicable to ordinary agricultural land.

The problems brought to law in connection with economic growth can be as great where men's hopes fail of realization as where they succeed. The costs—sometimes the fraud and sharp dealing—which accompany such failures pose particularly sharp questions concerning the relation of the legal order to economic processes. In the history of Wisconsin mineral exploitation, the search for gas and oil and the search for copper present two such instances.

The search for Wisconsin oil occurred shortly after the discovery of oil at Titusville, Pennsylvania, in 1859 and was spurred by the great public demand for oil products. By 1865 oil fever in Wisconsin was running high. Companies were organized, geologists of "repute" made known their findings that oil was abundant, stock sales were brisk, and newspaper accounts were optimistic. For example, the editor of the *Green Bay Advocate* wrote: "Who knows but Northern Wisconsin may yet become a place of as much wealth and the scene of as much excitement as the oil regions of Pennsylvania now are."

Responding to the urge to get rich quickly, Wisconsin inhabitants invested untold thousands in ill-fated oil speculations. Estimates were that the 6,648 people of Madison invested $200,000.[11] This pattern was repeated the state over. Geologists informed the people that the oily blue scum on many marshes and lakes came from decaying organic matter and was not oil seepage from subterranean deposits. Such accurate knowledge did not stem the tide. Only expensive digging, which failed to produce a single gusher, did that. By late 1867 the craze was over, leaving many persons poorer but wiser, and reaffirming many a promoter's belief in the credulity of most people.

Subsequent to this post-Civil War activity oil fever occasionally flared up again, but no boom such as the 1867 episode repeated itself. In 1929 the State Geological Survey republished a paper entitled "The Negligible Oil and Gas Possibilities of Wisconsin." The title of the publication and its introductory remarks demonstrated that its purpose was to state facts about the subject to protect investors. The paper concluded that there was little likelihood of oil in Wisconsin, considering the geological history of the region.

Copper, like oil, whetted the gambling instinct and emptied the purses of many investors. Almost coincident with the opening of the lead region, miners reported finding evidence of copper. In 1837 or 1838 some copper deposits were found a mile northeast of the Mineral Point courthouse, and the location was worked until 1842. From 1873 to 1875, two hundred tons of copper were mined around Mineral Point. During the Civil War period $45,000 was spent in Douglas County without much success. Newspapers frequently carried optimistic articles like this from the *Appleton Crescent:* "A large portion of our county is underlied with rich copper beds, almost, if not quite equal to the Lake Superior region!" [12]

Northern Wisconsin was the scene of most copper activity in the post-Civil War period. During the late 1880's and at the beginning of the twentieth century, spurts of activity occurred. Of the efforts of the eighties the geological survey stated that a large portion of $100,000 spent was "not judiciously expended" because "the occurrence of the metal, and the proper system of mining were [not] . . . well understood by anybody." [13]

Increased activity on Michigan copper ranges about 1900 produced action in Wisconsin. Wisconsin promoters hoped they could parallel Michigan success. At that time the geological survey reported: "It can be stated that in no place was a deposit of copper which was of sufficient richness shown to be of any great extent." [14] No discoveries up to 1950 challenged the correctness of this conclusion.

The processing or smelting phase of minerals played a less important role in Wisconsin's economy than did extraction or mining.

The regrettable fact was that Wisconsin had no coal or oil resources and thus totally lacked the fuel commonly used in smelting. Wood was used early in the history of the state, but it was less efficient than coal.

Prior to 1848 lead-region miners smelted large amounts of lead and what copper they found. Men failed in early attempts to smelt zinc shortly after 1848. Thereafter Wisconsin's zinc ore was transported outside the state for smelting, usually to Illinois. Much capital was invested in iron smelters. By 1859 the state possessed three charcoal blast furnaces—at Mayville in Dodge County, at Ironton in Sauk County, and at Black River Falls in Jackson County. The 1860 United States census credited Wisconsin with producing two thousand tons of pig iron. By 1865 the furnace at Black River Falls had failed but another at Iron Ridge, Dodge County, kept the total figure at three. By 1870 the state's iron-smelting industry had developed on a sturdy basis. In that year the Milwaukee Iron Company completed new rolling mills which were reported to be the largest in the country. An 1876 publication listed eleven blast furnaces operating in the state; nine used charcoal and two coke and anthracite.[15] Despite a limited smelting industry, the state managed to build some impressive factories which used iron and steel. Especially noteworthy were the farm machinery factories, where such names as Van Brunt, Deering, McCormick, John Deere, and J. I. Case loomed large.

This, then, was the physical and economic setting within which unfolded the legal history of mineral development in Wisconsin. It is time now to focus upon the law. The law was, indeed, part of the story—not simply to keep order, but also to provide a formal framework for action, and beyond that in a measure to foster and promote and to regulate action. Lawyers were in the story too. In 1837 Mineral Point had six lawyers—more than in 1959. They were busy people. "The numerous quarrels about mines, the jumping of claims, the encroachment of diggers upon each other, caused endless litigation presenting a fruitful field for the exercise of the talents of the lawyer."[16]

Many of the legal problems were settled by compromises and adjustments that left no public record. The significance of these to society, past and present, is lost, but scores of conflicts were settled only after legislation, speeches, court suits, and reports were placed upon public record. The public record of the problems and their adjustment provides the raw material for the chapters which follow.

2

Uncle Sam: Landlord

ONE OF THE great compromises by which a loose confederation of states became a nation was consummated when Virginia in 1784 and other states within a few years ceded to the United States in Congress assembled their claims to the area which includes today's Wisconsin. The surrender of the western land claims of the original states placed in the national government the ownership of immense real wealth through which it possessed unique opportunity and responsibility to influence the growth of the country. An important part of the assets of which the United States was now proprietor was the mineral wealth of this land. Should it be leased? Sold? Husbanded? Worked by the national government? Given the size of the stakes, decisions on issues like these could materially affect the nature of the economy, the balance of political power, and even the general value pattern of the culture for many years to come.

Several provisions of the great Survey Ordinance of 1785 suggested bold use of this national ownership. Consistent with the high value society in 1785 put on private property and the market, as institutions under which men might freely exercise their power, the major policy reflected by the ordinance was sale of the public land into private fee simple ownership. The survey created by the 1785 ordinance was intended primarily to implement this basic objective. Thus, it is the more striking that the ordinance made certain distinct provisions as to mineral wealth. First, there was indication that the public lands be classified in terms of their special features of natural wealth. The ordinance instructed the federal surveyors to note upon the plats, "all mines, salt springs, salt licks and mill seats" which they observed. In a second, and more positive, stipulation the ordinance provided: "There shall be reserved . . . one-third part of all gold, silver, lead and copper mines, to be sold, or otherwise disposed of as Congress shall hereafter direct." [1]

The ordinance's policy of identifying and reserving from sale the western lands containing minerals was motivated by at least three considerations. First, the policy was based upon historical precedent. In the early history of the common law in England ownership of all minerals belonged to the king, although gradually under mounting pressures this broad sovereign claim declined until it applied only to gold and silver. An unpopular court decision in 1568 which upheld the king's right to *all* minerals when mixed with gold and silver was soon changed by an Act of Parliament.[2] Despite this dilution of the royal right at home, English kings and queens continued to reserve for the Crown various kinds of minerals found in the New World. Many colonial charters, such as the royal grants to Sir Walter Raleigh and Lord Baltimore, provided that a percentage of minerals should belong to the Crown.[3]

Second, in 1785 minerals, especially lead, bore directly upon the nation's ability to defend itself from attack. Revolutionary War mineral shortages so severe that lead in windows was extracted and turned into bullets were yet vivid memories. Unsettled international conditions forced such statesmen as Thomas Jefferson to think seriously about the discovery, ownership, and development of a national supply of minerals.

Lastly, and not unrelated to the tie between an effective defense establishment and an adequate mineral supply, was domestic concern over the evil possibility of monopoly. This threat emanated from the nature of mineral wealth. Vital to self-defense as well as to domestic progress, limited in quantity and concentrated in location, minerals offered a foundation upon which might be founded monopolistic power in economic areas of immense public concern.

Until Congress enacted the first comprehensive leasing law in 1807 there existed only a vague federal policy for the mineral lands reserved by the ordinance of 1785. In 1796 Congress directed federal surveyors to note in their field books "the true situation of all mines"; and in 1800 Congress delegated power to the surveyor general to lease the "lands of the United States reserved for future disposition" [4] with leases not exceeding seven years. Although lead lands were not expressly mentioned, properly interpreted the act would embrace the lead lands because they were "lands of the United States reserved for future disposition." No lead-land leases authorized by this law have been discovered.

The significance of the lack of a complete federal policy for the reserved mineral lands became apparent shortly after Jefferson overrode his own doubts about the constitutionality of his action and purchased Louisiana from Napoleon in 1803. This purchase brought into United States ownership a vast territory that included the lead lands of Missouri. On the date the purchase was consummated, many miners were working Missouri lead lands. It was clear to federal leaders that continued lack of definite federal policy for the lead lands in Missouri would be calamitous. If positive steps were not taken to implement the reservation policy, to do something with the reserved lands, and to provide rules under which the miners already at work could continue, the wealth of the Missouri mines would be lost to the nation forever. The formulation of a policy for the Missouri mines was complicated by the fact that a considerable number of miners were operating under grants from the previous owners, France and Spain. These miners did not consider themselves trespassers. Many of their titles and possessory claims were based upon documents and records that were for the most part authentic.

A provision of the Louisiana Purchase treaty with France specified that the United States should protect the inhabitants in the free enjoyment of their property. Pursuant to this commitment, Congress established in 1805 a commission to adjust conflicting claims to land in the area. Under the law three appointed agents represented the interests of the United States before the commission. The law directed the agents to

examine into and investigate the titles and claims, if any there be, to the lead mines, . . . to collect all the evidence . . . with respect to the claims to, and value of the said mines, and to lay the same before the commissioners, who shall make a special report thereof, . . . to the Secretary of the Treasury to be by him laid before Congress, at their next ensuing session.[5]

The commissioners and the agents labored diligently to unsnarl the conflicting grants, but the goal was impossible to achieve. By 1811 the magnitude and complexities of the problem dictated a complete cessation of attempts to settle private differences and at the same time to protect the mineral title of the United States. The efforts of the commissioners and agents were largely neutral in the impact upon federal lead-land policy.

In 1807 Congress passed a comprehensive piece of legislation affecting the lead lands. This enactment established a policy of management which was to remain the cornerstone of legislation on lead mines as long as federal ownership was retained. The law provided

that the several lead mines . . . , together with as many sections contiguous to each as shall be deemed necessary by the President of the United States, shall be reserved for the future disposition of the United States; and any grant which may hereafter be made for a tract of land containing a lead mine, which had been discovered previous to the purchase of such tract from the United States, shall be considered fraudulent and null; and the President of the United States shall be, and is hereby authorized to lease any lead mine which has been or may hereafter be discovered . . . , for a term not exceeding five years.[6]

This law contained three basic policy decisions. First, Congress prohibited sale of all lead lands in the public domain, together with other lands deemed necessary to the development of the lead deposits. This extended the policy of the 1785 ordinance which reserved only one-third part. Second, the act authorized short-term leases of the lead lands thus reserved. Lastly, the law sought to protect federal reservations by stipulating that all sales of federal land should be void if at the time of the sale the purchaser knew, or had reason to know, that the land contained lead. That the law applied only to lead and was silent about federal policy with respect to other minerals is explained by the importance of lead as war matériel and by the fact that congressional attention was drawn to lead through the existence of the producing Missouri deposits.

Pursuant to the delegation of authority contained in the 1807 law, President Thomas Jefferson assigned Frederick Bates the duty of superintending the federal mines and enforcing the federal leasing program. Bates immediately went to Missouri, the only area with lead mines operating at the time. There he met a cool, and in some cases hostile, reception. Shortly after his arrival Bates notified the miners of the purpose of his mission: to issue leases on federally owned lead mines and to collect rent from the leaseholders. From the miner's viewpoint, laws requiring them to procure a license and pay a fee for the privilege of digging lead were unnecessary and void because for many years under claims of right stemming from old Spanish and French grants they had carried on such activity without paying tribute. Miners who did avail themselves of leases found Bates powerless to place and keep them in possession of the leaseholds. Those who took leases and obtained peaceful possession of the granted lands commonly did not honor their promises to pay rent.[7]

Bates's inability to administer the leasing system in Missouri rested upon several points. First, the federal leasing policy was tardy in appearance. By 1807 an entirely contrary plan of ownership of the Missouri lead mines had grown to maturity. Bates's problem was not solely to introduce new federal policy, but to displace an old, established system of ownership. The existing system was radically unlike the new federal policy, since the old practice rested upon concepts and values of private property, enforced and supplemented by almost universal adherence to mining customs. Customs such as the one which permitted a miner who struck a vein to follow it twenty-five feet in all directions without interference already pro-

vided workable rules founded upon common acceptance and origi-
nating with the governed group. To expect a lone federal officer to
displace such a system was to demand the impossible.

Second, no court system respected by the miners existed to force
adherence to the law Bates was charged with enforcing. Legal
procedures were handicapped because the court machinery tradi-
tionally used in enforcing such laws was in the hands of individuals
sympathetic to the miners. To rely upon local jurors to enforce
federal policy would have been futile. Men sympathetic to the miners'
arguments occupied other seats of power within the judicial structure, if not on the bench, at least in the offices important for enforcing court orders.

Lastly, the use of military force to assist Bates was out of the
question. Soon after Bates assumed his duties the nation's war resources were directed to the external problem of asserting freedom
of the seas from British interference. But even had the War of 1812
not broken out, the issues in Missouri were not serious enough to
warrant the drastic remedy of military intervention.

From 1812 to 1816 matters drifted while the United States directed
its attention to fighting a war. In 1812 Congress created the General
Land Office, and assigned the task of administering the leasing
system to the new agency. Bates continued to administer the program in Missouri. In 1816 he reported that he had gathered $1,622
in rent—the first rent he had reported. On November 21, 1821,
President Monroe transferred administration of the leasing system
to the War Department. The record does not disclose the reasons
for this change. Lead was then considered primarily war matériel;
probably the President decided that administration of a war resource
belonged more properly in the War Department than in the Treasury
Department.

The War Department immediately assigned to George Bomford
of the Ordnance Bureau the task of overseeing the leasing program
in Missouri. When he assumed his duties, Bomford found no leases
in existence. This fact demonstrates the failure of federal policy to
that date. About this time Henry Schoolcraft toured the Missouri

mines and reported to President Monroe that the federal policy suffered because no skilled mineralogist headed the program. There is reason to suppose that Schoolcraft had in mind a qualified candidate for Superintendent of the Lead Mines and that the candidate was himself. On December 3, 1822, President Monroe suggested to Congress that provision for a superintendent might benefit the program.[8] Monroe did not name any individual for the position, and Congress took no action. On his own authority the President then appointed Lieutenant Martin Thomas Superintendent of the Lead Mines.

Lieutenant Thomas re-examined the entire federal reservation and leasing program to draft needed changes in administration for efficiency. First, he concluded that there was a basic practical block to effective reservation of lead lands from sale because lead-bearing lands were not easily identified. Government surveyors running township lines noted in their books any surface features which indicated that lead might be present, but employees running section lines made no similar record. Observations of surface features based upon six-mile intervals were almost useless. No scientific survey of the Missouri mining area had been undertaken. Government officials on the scene in Missouri, such as Bates, were too few and too preoccupied with other duties to examine all of the land in the mining area.

The consequence of this lack of information was that officials could not prove whether lead ore came from reserved government land or from privately owned land. Property rights in lead lands held under valid Spanish or French grants were protected by the treaty, and the universal defense to a demand for federal rent was that the lead came from private lands.

Thomas observed, further, that federal officials were too few to investigate each individual miner to ascertain the source of his lead. Many miners took lead from federal lands without color of title. They sold the lead to smelters, who later shipped it eastward. Much of this traffic went on without the knowledge of federal officials, and, what with the size of the problem and the want of staff, no effective means existed for federal officials to discover the facts.

After full consideration of these handicaps, Thomas devised and instituted a new plan for collecting rent. By this time a considerable number of smelteries had sprung up. Thomas ordered each smelter to obtain a license. This license granted the right to buy lead ore from federal mines, conditional upon the smelter's paying to the United States 10 per cent of the lead as a rental fee. Each licensee-smelter was bonded to insure the claim of the United States to its 10 per cent. Although the rent was collected from the smelter, there was no doubt that the smelter would pass the charge on to the miner by an appropriate reduction in the purchase price of the ore. Each smelter-licensee agreed not to buy lead ore dug from federal land without consent of the government lessee. This provision was designed to penalize miners who trespassed on federal property and ousted the rightful federal leaseholder. To cover miners who still smelted their own ore, Thomas continued to grant old-style leases.[9]

Thomas's plan met some, but not all, of the difficulties that had long plagued federal policy. One advantage of his program was that to some extent it mollified the people actually paying the tax. Missouri miners did not look kindly upon a rule requiring payment of rent. By assessing smelters in lieu of miners, Thomas's program blunted the imposition of the tax and reduced the animosity which miners had toward the whole program of federal ownership and leasing. Another advantage was that smelters were less mobile than miners: a smelter generally located and kept his works near a good supply of wood for fuel. Collecting taxes from smelters also promised to be more efficient because there were many fewer smelters than miners.

However, one basic difficulty remained unsolved under Thomas's plan. Smelters were in no better position to know the source of the ore they purchased than were federal officials. Private titles to lead lands existed because of property rights protected by the treaty, and also because under the language of the 1807 leasing law, private sales could be voided only if the purchaser knew at the time of the sale that the land was lead bearing. With no accurate scientific test to locate lead ore in place and no staff to survey the hundreds of acres of Missouri lands, nothing prevented sales of land which later turned out to be lead bearing. No amount of clever administrative improvising could change this situation.

By 1827 Thomas's reports showed plainly that he was discouraged over results. Smelters sent very little lead to federal depots. Smelters and miners colluded. Some smelters defied federal authority by refusing to take out licenses or to make required reports. In 1826, 112,560 pounds of lead rent came from the Missouri mines and in 1827, 44,467 pounds, but there is no way to estimate the amount that should have been paid. Federal officials soon found the problem expanding as Missouri miners, as well as others, began migrating up the Mississippi to the Fever River mines in Illinois. A little later men invaded an area which would later lie within the boundaries of Wisconsin. Existing federal personnel, already overburdened with the Missouri part of the program, were assigned supervision of the new area. A final accounting for the Missouri mines from 1821 to 1829 shows that $12,688.49 in rent lead was collected at a cost of $9,175.60, leaving a net gain to landlord Uncle Sam of $3,512.89.[10]

At the same time that Lieutenant Thomas and Bates were meeting insurmountable administrative difficulties, Congress began to show discontent with the federal lead-lands policy. As early as 1812 Representative Morrow of Ohio presented a bill "concerning the lead mines in the Territory of Missouri." The bill died quickly. In 1815 the House of Representatives appointed a special committee "to inquire into the expediency of better regulating by law, the working and leasing the public lead mines in the Territory of Missouri, in such manner as to secure the lessees in the quiet enjoyment of their leases and to enable the Government to collect its rent."[11] This special committee presented a bill, which was not enacted. Nonetheless, the charge which Congress thus laid upon the committee, to inquire into the lack of protection of lessees and the failure to collect rent, showed that some congressmen were aware of the state of affairs in Missouri.

In the Thirteenth and Fourteenth Congresses (1813–1815 and 1815–1817), Rufus Eaton, delegate from Missouri Territory, spearheaded efforts to move Congress to act on the Missouri lead-lands problem. He persuaded the Fourteenth Congress to pass a resolution directing that the House committee on public lands make the same inquiry as the special committee of 1815. Eaton presented a resolution from the Missouri Territorial Legislature concerning the lead mines, and he induced Congress to require the Secretary of the Treasury to collect and submit to the next session all facts in his office relative to the management of the Missouri lead lands. This information was presented to the following session of Congress, but again nothing more than passage of a resolution directing the committee on public lands to investigate the matter was achieved. Eaton's efforts never progressed beyond resolutions to secure information on the operation of the 1807 act.

In the Fifteenth Congress, John Scott, delegate from Missouri, assumed the responsibility for goading Congress to act. His first request was identical with previous ones—a resolution directing the public lands committee to investigate. His second request differed greatly from previous moves. He requested examination of the possibility that the federal government should dispose of such lead lands as were "deemed not of sufficient extent or value to be retained." This was the first official hint that any member of Congress thought it proper to re-examine the basic premise of the 1807 leasing law—the wisdom of federal ownership. All previous moves were in the direction of investigating the leasing situation with the idea of perfecting it by protecting government lessees and by removing the reasons for non-payment of rent. Scott's resolution suggested doubts about the purpose and efficacy of the 1807 law.

Matters remained static until the second session of the Seventeenth Congress in January, 1823. Missouri had then become a state entitled to full representation in the Senate of the United States. Probably there never existed a more avowed and active protagonist for the interests of his constituency than one of the men Missouri sent to Washington to speak for the state. This man was Thomas Hart Benton, born in North Carolina of scholarly and well-to-do parents, school teacher, farmer, lawyer, and politician, who during his thirty years in the United States Senate put into eloquent and ringing speeches the inner feelings of the West. Long remembered as the man who dedicated himself to destroying the second Bank of the United States, Benton was no less eager to put an end to government ownership of the mines of Missouri. His views on government mineral ownership were so strongly stated that they remained to do yeoman service at a later date when the same questions were raised concerning Wisconsin lead lands.

The slavery issue was temporarily quiet as a result of the Missouri Compromise. Only seven years had run under the twenty-year charter of the second Bank of the United States. Thus, Benton could readily concentrate his energies upon the reserved lead lands, which he considered as standing athwart the development of the West.

On January 21, 1823, Senator Benton reported to the Senate a bill which authorized the President to cause the lead lands to be placed on public sale. The *Annals of Congress* report that Senator Benton "delivered himself" of a long speech supporting his bill. He expounded upon the richness of the mines of Missouri; he recited their history; he enumerated the laws passed to perfect federal ownership. He characterized the leasing system as a "luminous" idea, which had turned the nation into a "landlord, the miners into national tenants." He summed up the result: "What has been the fruit of this monopolizing and leasing system? Have any leases been taken? Yes, many. Has any lead been dug? Yes, many millions of pounds weight. Have any rents been paid? No, not a dollar—not one cent." [12]

Benton went on to say that if financial gain were the purpose of federal ownership, the leasing system was a failure. If the proponents of the leasing system thought the policy would encourage western development, they were mistaken because the result was quite the contrary. The 1807 policy was evil because Missouri miners were motivated to take only the easily secured ores near the surface. Missouri miners were "picking at the eyes of the mine," because only a fee owner would invest money to sink shafts and explore for ore at the lower levels. According to Benton, a spirit of tenantry was adverse to the permanent settlements which the West desperately needed.

Benton was striking to obtain a completely new federal policy, not merely to patch holes in the 1807 law. Admittedly, some defects in the old policy could be cleared by new legislation, but Benton was "against the leasing system," because it was wrong "in its first principles." The senator not only doubted the wisdom of federal ownership, but also questioned its constitutional base. It was his opinion that the Constitution gave Congress power to create a "transient trustee-possession," but denied Congress the power to create any system of "permanent ownership." Benton prophesied that continuation of the program would turn the federal government into a "petty landlord" demanding a tithe from its vassals and ever ready to use the legal remedy of distress for collection of arrearages in rent. The results would be: "Population retarded, the improvement of the country delayed, large bodies of land held free of taxation, and . . . decisions more or less influenced by the presence of men holding their leases at the will of the Federal Government." [13]

The senator had no doubt about what the future policy should be. The only true course was for the people to throw off this "intervention of a foreign government." Congress should return the mines to the people, who by their individual initiative and enterprise would develop them as the British owners of the soil had developed the rich copper mine of Anglesea and the vast salt mine of Cheshire. Any other course would cause the bulk of the minerals to go undiscovered and the area to remain unsettled.

Senator Benton's proposal represented a drastic change in federal policy as it had existed since enactment of the 1807 leasing law. It was not to be expected that the Benton bill would win quick or easy approval. That the subject was seen to be important was shown when ten senators rose to speak after Benton had finished. At a later date the bill was laid on the table and remained there. The Senate was uncertain about the value of the federal lead mines. Though Congress had passed many resolutions seeking to obtain information on the subject, it still had no report or tabulation upon which to base an over-all value. This was understandable; no survey of the Missouri mines had been made and no person could gauge accurately the number of acres of lead-bearing land or the quantity or quality of ore they contained.

One fact was clear after Senator Benton had finished: he would lead the push to repeal the 1807 law. And in this man the forces opposed to federal ownership possessed a sagacious and persuasive leader. Never once did the senator discuss or dispute the two strong considerations behind the 1807 law—fear of monopoly and assurance of vital war matériel.

While Benton boldly urged in the Senate that the Missouri lead lands should be sold, House action followed the old familiar pattern of seeking information. A resolution was passed asking the President to furnish data on the number of mines, the number of leases and their terms. When the information was slow in coming, the House asked that it be furnished to the next session. The resolutions make clear that the House still sought a way to perfect the system of government ownership.

At the next session of Congress (December, 1823–May, 1824), Senator Benton, ably assisted by his colleague from Missouri, Senator Barton, renewed his assault upon government ownership. These two men assessed the chances of their proposal and determined that although they could enlist a considerable number of Senate votes, many senators, mostly from the eastern states, were less ardent about the proposal. Much of this lack of enthusiasm stemmed from uncertainty about the value of the federal property which Benton and Barton desired to sell. Many senators deemed such facts essential if the United States was to receive a fair value. To satisfy some senators on this score, Barton offered a resolution asking that the committee on public lands consider the expediency of selling the mines and the need for enacting some provision for spreading knowledge among the people before the sale. The committee dispatched a request to the Treasury Department asking for information, but the reply arrived too late in the session to permit preparation of a bill.

Several sessions yet remained before Senators Benton and Barton calculated they had the votes needed to pass a sale bill, but in the interval they were not quiet. In one session Senator Benton discovered that the officer in charge of the federal lead lands had collected rent in lead worth $2,000, and being unable to find any provision in the law on the point, was asking what disposition he should make of the lead. Senator Benton introduced a bill authorizing the President to grant $2,000 worth of lead belonging to the United States to build a road from a lead mine in Missouri to the Mississippi River. The senator argued that if the rent lead was not disposed of in this manner, there was nothing else to do with it except to ship it to a federal arsenal, the nearest of which was a thousand miles distant. Benton conveniently overlooked the fact that other Missouri lead owners had no difficulty selling their lead on the spot. Nothing further was done about the bill.

At the session following the defeat of his road bill, Senator Benton vigorously pushed the idea of selling the Missouri lead lands. He burst into action when the Senate committee on public lands recommended indefinite postponement of a bill authorizing the President to sell the mines. Lack of evidence about the value of the lead mines was the reason given by the committee. Benton informed the Senate that he was disgusted because his efforts were always sidetracked by the specious argument that the "time was not suitable" for his bill. He reiterated his argument that the whole system was unconstitutional. He railed against the reservation policy, which by now, he said, was applied to 660,000 acres, many of them fertile farm land. Sometimes he overlooked historical facts, as he did when he suggested that the Founding Fathers would have "scouted the idea of making the Federal Government a lead-mine digger." He scoffed at the idea that there was a lack of information on the value of the mines. He maintained that numerous reports to the federal government included more than enough information to enable a senator to cast an intelligent vote. He was definitely against any more delay for the purpose of securing additional information. When a senator suggested that the information should be gathered for the benefit of the President so that he would not be placed in the position of selling a federal pig in a poke, Benton replied that there were already five hundred pages on the subject, and ignored the reply that the number of pages was not always a test of the accuracy or usefulness of a report. Senator Johnson of Kentucky supported Benton's idea: the "nation had become too much like a counting-house, . . . and whenever he found an opportunity to lop off any of the branches of the business of this counting-house he was disposed to do so." [14] Although Benton was gaining support for his measure, on January 10, 1827, the bill was again laid on the table.

However, Senator Benton was on the verge of success. At the second session of the Twentieth Congress (December, 1828–March, 1829), he introduced a bill to sell the lead lands. Senatorial debate brought out nothing new. In fact, compared to all the oratory before, this debate was most quiet. The bill passed both houses of Congress and was approved by President Adams on March 3, 1829.[15] The next morning, March 4, 1829, Senator Benton had two reasons to be happy as an old man in a simple black suit and a cravat of the same hue became the new President of the United States; the West and the common people could breathe a little easier, secure in the knowledge that the executive power rested in the hands of "Andy" Jackson and that Congress had authorized the sale of the Missouri lead lands.

Benton's law authorized the President to cause the lead lands of Missouri which were "unclaimed by individuals" to be sold at any time the President thought proper. The bill provided for six months' notice of the sale so that the public might be informed of the location of the mines, the possibility of finding ore, the quality of the ore, and the facilities for manufacturing the lead into useful commodities. Senator Benton's law dealt with the Missouri lead mines only. In fact, one of his main arguments for the bill was that the upper Mississippi lead mines were far more valuable and that the government, therefore, did not need to retain the Missouri mines. Benton's pride in the Missouri mines must have suffered a little when events forced him to argue that they were not as valuable as those up the river. But the concession was necessary to get his bill enacted. In this cause, evidently, he was willing to belittle somewhat mines which several years earlier he had assured the Senate were the most valuable ever known, needing only individual initiative and private ownership to develop.

One of the complaints from Missouri had been that patents were withheld from persons who purchased land which later proved to be lead bearing. The third section of Benton's law took care of this complaint by providing that patents should be issued to these persons "as in ordinary cases . . . of sales."

President Jackson immediately caused the lead lands of Missouri to be put upon the block, and they were sold. If we include both the lead lands and the acres reserved because of the location of salt springs, 2,800 square miles of federally reserved lands were located in Missouri. The lead lands were sold at an average price of $1.28 per acre, one cent above the average price received by the federal government for ordinary public land. Thus ended the federal reservation of Missouri lead lands.

Congress had indeed lopped off one branch of the business of the "counting-house," but Uncle Sam remained a lead-land proprietor with holdings in Illinois and in Michigan Territory. The harassed Superintendent of the Lead Mines still stood charged with enforcing the 1807 leasing law in those areas. The first leases in the upper Mississippi region had been granted in 1822, and when Lieutenant Thomas arrived in 1825, he had found many miners at work, mostly without a federal license. By 1827 or 1828 somewhere between 2,000 and 3,500 miners were at work, chiefly around Galena, Illinois, which was the center of the area because of its favorable location for water transportation on the Fever and Mississippi rivers. It was not long until these miners spread northward into land which was to be Wisconsin. They encroached upon Indian lands as they did so, for it was not until 1829 that the United States signed treaties with the Chippewa, Ottawa, Potawatomi, and Winnebago tribes giving the United

States title to the land south of the Wisconsin River which came to be known as the lead region.

Thomas had added some refinements to his administrative machinery. He continued to issue licenses to smelters, but he also required individual miners to secure permits authorizing the holder to mine on federal land. Permit holders agreed to begin mining in nine days; smelters agreed not to buy lead except from a permit holder; no miner might hold two permits; rent was still collected from the smelters. There is evidence that some roving permits were issued, authorizing the holder to dig ore anywhere. This innovation resulted from the miners' habit of prospecting over large areas and their dislike of a permit system which tied them to a single plot.

The hostility of the miners to federal ownership was clearly evident, but many secured permits: 2,133 permits were issued in 1827. In 1829 Lieutenant Thomas was replaced by Thomas McKnight, whose tenure lasted one year, and then by Thomas Legate. Senator Benton may have played a major role in Thomas's discharge. Thomas's energetic administration of the leasing program, it seems, may have occasioned Benton's displeasure. Superintendent Legate introduced certain modifications that pleased the miners. In 1830 he reduced the rent from 10 to 6 per cent, and he announced that he would not enforce the permit provision prohibiting the farming of federal land.

Administration of the leasing program in Missouri was seriously hampered from the beginning because the existence of large tracts of privately owned lead lands made proof that specific lead ore was dug from federal lands almost impossible. Prior to 1834 no corresponding situation troubled the program in Wisconsin. In Wisconsin and Illinois no treaty-protected Spanish and French grants clouded the United States title. Because no Wisconsin federal lands had been sold, all lands, mineral and non-mineral alike, belonged to the United States. All who dug ore on these lands without United States permission were trespassers.

The unquestioned title of the United States to all Wisconsin lead lands was soon to be disturbed. On June 26, 1834, President Jackson approved a bill which provided:

That the President shall be authorized . . . to cause to be offered for sale . . . all the land . . . (lying north of Illinois, west of Lake Michigan and south and east of the Fox and Wisconsin Rivers) reserving only section sixteen in each township, . . . and such reservation as the President shall deem necessary for military posts, any law of Congress heretofore existing to the contrary notwithstanding.[16]

The President immediately exercised the power granted in this act. His proclamation authorizing the sale provided: "All tracts of land on which lead mines . . . are indicated . . . by the plats . . . together with such tracts as from satisfactory evidence to be adduced by the Register of the Land Office . . . shall be shown to contain a lead mine, shall be excluded from the sale." [17]

The act established two land offices in Wisconsin: the westernmost was at Mineral Point, the other at Green Bay. Mineral Point was the designated place where sales of federal land located in the lead area would be conducted, purchase money received, and records listing the reserved federal lands in the lead district made and preserved. President Jackson appointed John P. Shelton, a loyal Jacksonian Democrat, as first register of the Mineral Point Land Office.

The Presidential proclamation issued pursuant to the 1834 act placed squarely upon the register's shoulders the duty of reserving federal lead lands from sale. Shelton used three methods to identify federal lead lands. First, he refused to sell any lands which federal surveyors noted as lead bearing. Evidence indicates that federal surveyors were not too diligent in looking for evidence of ore upon the land they were traversing. Second, he restricted from sale all lands which the Superintendent of the Lead Mines requested to have reserved. There is little evidence that Legate, or any of the superintendents who followed him in that office, spent much time searching for lead lands to be reserved in the name of the federal government. Third, he reserved lands in cases in which information of their lead-bearing character was brought to his attention. Even though this multiplicity of methods existed, reservation was haphazard and rested to a great extent in the hands of persons unskilled in even the rudiments of geology.

The register of the Mineral Point Land Office occupied a key position to influence reservation of federal lead lands. He actually entered the notations on the plat books and other records which preserved the federal property. To discover and preserve lead-bearing lands for the federal government, Shelton required that each person applying to buy federal land in his district produce two witnesses to swear that they were acquainted with the land and that there were "no discoveries of ore thereon, and that the tract . . . [was] not occupied by any smelter of lead ore."

The register improvised this technique of the "Shelton Oath" without any specific delegation of power from Congress. But the procedure could be justified as a necessary formulation of rules to aid the register to carry out his assigned duties. Far from the Wisconsin lead area and without facts, Congress and the President could only sketch federal policy in broad strokes, leaving field administrators to issue rules and define procedures to implement policy. In the hands of a wise and trustworthy official, the existence of this power provided flexibility to meet changing conditions and allowed for experiment to find workable procedures, but in the hands of a less honorable person such power opened avenues for wrongdoing ranging from minor peculation to wholesale fraud.

Whether to characterize Shelton's administration of the office of register of the Mineral Point Land Office as rotten and corrupt or only as naive and gullible, presents a difficult choice over one hundred years later. Certain facts are undisputed and they are important since they had real impact on federal reservation of Wisconsin lead lands. First, many acres of lead-bearing lands were sold to private individuals who applied to Shelton at the Mineral Point Land Office. Second, many of these purchasers used illegal means to procure these sales. Among the deceitful practices employed to purchase federal lead lands was one designed to circumvent Shelton's requirement that a prospective purchaser produce the affidavits of two persons that they knew the land the purchaser sought to buy, and that, to their knowledge, it was not lead bearing. Many times affiants were conducted blindfolded over the land to ease their consciences when they swore that they had been over the land and that to their knowledge it did not contain lead. If the purchaser did not desire to go to this trouble he could procure two persons willing to swear falsely. The effectiveness of the oath was completely destroyed when a United States court sitting at Mineral Point refused to find false swearing under the Shelton oath perjurious on the ground that the oath itself was not authorized by law.

A second trick commonly used was for the purchaser to engage an accomplice to divert the register's attention from the books while Shelton's penciled notations designating reserved lead lands were neatly erased.

Although Shelton may have been an innocent dupe in these frauds, he participated actively in another procedure which violated the spirit and probably also the letter of the law. Longstanding policy was that no federal land be opened to private entry until after the land had been offered at public auction. Shelton evaded this policy by the most transparent formalism in disposing of federal mineral land. Upon the purported public offering of all the federal lands in an area, Shelton refused bids for lands which he declared reserved as mineral bearing. Nonetheless, he construed the public offering as including the reserved lands, and ruled that after the auction the reserved lands were subject to private entry if they were then deemed not to bear minerals. To determine whether a tract bore minerals, Shelton invoked his oath procedure.

All contemporary proceedings to inquire into Shelton's knowledge of these illegal acts were afflicted with political overtones. Thus, the results were flavored to meet the tastes of the political party conducting the investigation. In 1837 the Whigs failed in an attempt to indict Shelton after numerous rumors were spread that the register was misusing his office to the advantage of Jacksonian Democrats and the severe disadvantage of Whigs. A federal examiner's report of the same year found irregularities and methods of keeping records which the examiner could not approve, but he decided that Shelton had not benefited personally, and he recommended that Shelton be retained.

When James Doty, Whig, replaced George Jones, Democrat, in 1839 as territorial delegate in Washington, a new move to investigate Shelton was initiated. Shelton's office was investigated by Moses M. Strong, United States District Attorney, but the report of the investigation mentioned only irregularities and loose methods of conducting business. Strong's report placed the blame upon people who were base enough to take advantage of Shelton and to lie in order to buy land.

In October, 1840, President Van Buren removed Shelton from office. But damage to the federal policy during Shelton's tenure was irreparable. Some estimates are that as much as two-thirds of the total area of lead-bearing lands passed into private ownership during this period.[18] What public support the reservation program had, evaporated. The difficulties which had plagued federal officials in Missouri were repeated in Wisconsin. Smelters refused to pay rent to the United States, alleging that the lead they refined came from privately owned mines. The superintendent lacked the staff to investigate the source of lead ore. The United States withheld 566 patents from purchasers in cases where doubt existed about the procedures used to secure the land. Although the titles were imperfect without the patents, many of these tracts were sold several times. The withholding of patents by the government had no beneficial consequence upon the federal claim to the lead mines. Purchasers reasoned that if they could secure the right to the minerals against all other miners, the existence of a paramount federal title mattered little. Many miners proceeded to take the minerals as quickly as possible, and after they had accomplished that, cared little about ownership of the land itself.

While Shelton's inept handling of the business of the Mineral Point Land Office continued, the office of Superintendent of the Lead Mines passed through the hands of a number of men, most of whom were desultory in administering the law. In 1837 Legate left office after both he and his superior, Colonel Bomford, Chief of Ordnance, had concluded that the best policy would be to sell the lands. Legate's successor, John H. Weber, lasted until 1841; Henry King then took office, to be followed by John Flanagan, who was removed in 1844 for mishandling federal funds. Successive holders were Major John Floyd, John McLenmore, and finally James Mitchell. Colonel Bomford, in charge of the lead mines since 1821 as Chief of Ordnance, gave way to Colonel Talcott in 1839.

Personnel changes were never accompanied by much variation in administration. Outside of some success by Flanagan, who issued a large number of permits during his tenure, miners almost entirely stopped applying for permits. Lead rent began declining in 1833, and in 1836 there is no record that any rent was collected. As the table on page 40 shows, after 1836 the United States had very little success in collecting rent.

At the time Flanagan held office, the development in the mining area of a new class of owners induced some miners to secure federal permits. By 1840, through fraudulent practices in the Mineral Point Land Office and in some instances through purchases of land where later lead was discovered, many acres of lead lands found their way into private ownership. Ownership of much of this acreage was soon concentrated in a relatively few men, many of whom were absentee owners. Wandering miners disliked these private owners, who often charged a higher rent than the federal government.

Sentiment against speculators and absentee owners swept the ranks of the old-fashioned miners. Flanagan argued that the federal government was a more beneficent landlord than most of the private property owners. Miner publications went so far as to state that miners did not fear the relationship of landlord and tenant between the government and the people. Feeling that they would soon be driven from the area by the private landlords, wandering miners rushed to secure federal permits to give them a colorable claim to take ore.

Another factor motivating miners to apply for federal permits was the current thought that if Congress authorized sale of lead lands, the law might establish a preferred right to buy for the purchaser who already possessed a permit. Miners hoped that in this way they could successfully compete at the sale with speculators and secure title to their land. Without protection of this sort, they feared they would find themselves outbid at the sale and dispossessed of their holdings.

RENT—UPPER MISSISSIPPI AREA

Year	Rent Collected *	Unpaid Rent *
1826	85,880	
1827	518,218	
1828	1,100,581	
1829	1,268,366	65,736
1830	504,211	124,736
1831	271,627	172,207
1832		
1833	393,734	211,094
1834	335,084	328,802
1835	40,074	494,313
1836	None	
1837	None	
1838	30,000	
1839	None	
1840	None	
1841	None	
1842	30,942	524,963 †
1843	178,052	117,259
1844	17,000	
1845	None	
1846	None	

* Pounds of Lead.

† The United States in 1842 collected 49,901 pounds of lead and $1,808.14 in cash on old leases. There were still due 248,055 pounds of lead from smelters who had agreed to settle out of court.

Blank spaces indicate no information available.

Source: Facts gathered from Ann Keppel, "Attempts to Formulate and Administer a Federal Lead Land Policy" (Unpublished M.A. Thesis, University of Wisconsin, 1954).

Shelton's maladministration allowed sale of many acres of reserved lands, but only slowly. While this was occurring, a plan was formulated by Moses M. Strong and some others which would have divested the United States of its title to lead lands in one fell swoop. The plan was spectacular in scope and vision, and was based upon an ingenious argument possessing a semblance of logic.

Strong rested his theory on the traditional federal policy requiring a prior public offering before any federal land was subject to private sale. He argued that the public offering had been accomplished. He reasoned that in the 1834 act,[19] which opened Wisconsin land to buyers, Congress had ordered all the lands in the lead area of Wisconsin sold, because the act authorized the President to cause all lands in the area to be sold except certain lands, among which the reserved lead lands were not listed. Moses Strong concluded that this act "ordered" the President to sell all the lands—including lead lands—not specifically reserved, and that the act was a mandate to sell, not merely an authorization to the President to sell if he thought such action wise. In Strong's view the lead lands had been offered for public sale, had not been disposed of, and were subject to private entry at the minimum price of one dollar twenty-five cents per acre. If this legal reasoning was flawless, then all that remained was for a purchaser to tender the minimum price at the land office, whereupon it would be the duty of the register to issue the papers necessary to obtain the patent.

Strong needed financial and legal assistance to carry out his plan. The amount of money he would have needed to buy the lead lands of the United States in Wisconsin is difficult to determine because there are no reliable figures on the extent of the lead lands remaining after Shelton's tenure.[20] Strong enlisted the aid of Henry Hubbard of Charlestown, New Hampshire, to procure financing and to take steps to secure a favorable opinion from a high Washington official on the validity of the legal argument behind the operation. There is more than a suspicion that efforts were made to assure that a favorable opinion would be forthcoming from Washington. The favorable opinion was never rendered; in fact, the opposite occurred. On July 21, 1837, Attorney General B. F. Butler ruled that the 1834 act merely authorized the President to sell the lead lands if he thought best.

Further, the Attorney General ruled that there was language in the act which could be construed as a direction that the mineral lands should not be sold, even if the President thought that to do so would be the wise course.[21]

This opinion doomed the Strong plan. But Strong tendered a considerable amount of money to the Mineral Point Land Office register for specified tracts, and when the tender was refused, offered the same money over and over again for other specified tracts.

Concurrently with lethargic administration of the leasing program, loose handling of matters at the Mineral Point Land Office, and grandiose schemes to buy all reserved lead lands, congressmen from the upper Mississippi lead region pressed for sale of the remaining reserved acreage. As early as June 5, 1834, two hours of very animated discussion in the House of Representatives was touched off by a request from an Illinois representative that the members consider a bill authorizing sale of the lead lands in Michigan Territory. The Illinois representative, seconded by a Missourian, argued that to sell would be the best federal policy because the return from leasing was less than the expenses, and if the sale did not take place soon, the miners like so many moles would spoil the area for farming by throwing clay all over the fertile earth. Massachusetts' aged John Quincy Adams inquired whether the leases produced any revenue and observed that if not, they ought to, and that the difficulty was probably a simple case of rent not being paid. Ohio's Representative Vinton believed that the original purpose of the reservation was to prevent "immense individual monopolies," and that this purpose had been achieved. He warned, though, that the leasing system was destroying the short supply of timber in the area, but he failed to explain how private ownership of the lands would conserve this natural resource. He suggested that any sale bill should provide a six-month notice period during which eastern capitalists might arrange their investments to raise money necessary to buy land. The bill failed in the Senate, but the debate it provoked showed clearly that western congressmen faced some strong eastern opposition.

In addition to the east-west division of opinion concerning the best federal policy, two other major issues hampered speedy passage of a bill exposing Wisconsin lead lands to sale. Many lawmakers felt they had been required to legislate in the dark when sale of the Missouri lead lands was authorized. Apparently, many desired to follow a different course for the upper Mississippi area. Thus, a survey of the region was authorized, and geologist David Dale Owen was placed in charge. In November of 1839 Owen with 140 other men reached the mouth of the Rock River. While the boat carrying the survey party plowed northward on the Mississippi, Owen, assisted by one other professional geologist, held classes on board to train the rest of the group in elementary geology. Upon landing in the southern part of the lead region, the men spread out and started northward in a great wave across the region. As his employees trekked toward the Wisconsin River, Owen scurried about crossing and recrossing the region no less than eleven times, checking the progress and findings of the other men, and making on-the-spot examinations himself. Two months and six days, and one hundred thousand dollars later, the survey was completed. David Dale Owen wrote his account of the survey—the Owen Report.[22]

Unhappily, the fate of this report and the use made of it exemplified the characteristic weakness of the federal administration of the lead lands. Owen's manuscript report was elaborate and complete with maps and illustrations, but it was printed in an abridged and mutilated form, minus many important maps, and in insufficient quantity. The General Land Office failed to retain a single copy, and several years later paid a considerable sum for a reference copy after the book had become quite rare.

Congress refused several requests from the Commissioner of the General Land Office to reprint the book despite many unsatisfied demands for copies made upon the office and Owen. Within four years the government lost the original maps and illustrations submitted by Mr. Owen. Fortunately, Owen had duplicate copies which he made available. Finally the book was reprinted in 1844.[23]

Owen's conclusion that the area contained a lead supply which was "inexhaustible . . . for many years, if not for ages" buttressed the position of congressmen who argued that the government should not dispose of the valuable resource at less than its market value. The report worked against those who advocated sale of lead land at the same price as agricultural land.

Congressional opinion was divided over a second issue—if sale was ordered, should occupiers of the land be given a preference? The advocates of pre-emption argued that Owen's report made pre-emption necessary. Using the report, speculators could ascertain the location and extent of the valuable lead lands, and with these facts they would be in a better position to bid at the sales than would most of the miners who were probably unaware of the report, and certainly too busy to read and study it even if copies were available at Galena and Mineral Point. The major importance of the report's conclusion that the area contained an "inexhaustible" ore supply was in crystallizing opposition to sale of the lead lands at a low price per acre.

When Wisconsin achieved territorial status in 1836, the lead area gained official spokesmen in Washington. The territory's delegate could cite resolutions from the territorial legislature to witness home sentiment. With its large population and single economy, the lead region possessed the greatest bloc of political power in the territorial government.

A memorial to Congress proposed at the second session of Wisconsin's First Territorial Legislature (November, 1837–January, 1838) outlined what the miners wanted and articulated a position which remained unchanged until enactment of a sale bill. The basic premise of the memorial was that the miners had stronger claims to the land they were holding than any other class of settlers. The federal government, the argument ran, had invited miners to go upon the federal land by urging them to take permits from the federal government and to work the land. After this invitation many miners had established works of a permanent character and made valuable discoveries. These men had opened up the area; they had fought off the Indians; and they were entitled to a reward for their service in making other federal lands more valuable by providing a region safe for settlement. The memorial claimed that miners had paid more taxes, in the form of rent, than any other class and that the miners had had to buy all the provisions they needed because the leases and permits prohibited farming the land. The conclusion which the miners drew from these propositions was that the federal government should dispose of the lead lands, but under procedures whereby persons who were mining on federal land would secure it without competition from the larger purses of speculators.[24]

Later memorials dispatched to Washington contained similar proposals. The memorialists usually stressed the hardships suffered at the hands of Indians: one memorial recited that in 1832 the Indians surrounded the country on all sides, killing, scalping, and tomahawking many citizens. Pre-emption for miners was clearly favored in the territorial legislature. That the miners were "invitees" as distinguished from "squatters" was repeatedly asserted. Once a threat was made to revive Strong's argument that the lead lands had been "offered" for public sale by the 1834 act and were thereafter available for private entry without need of further federal legislation.

But despite strong pleas from the territory for a sale bill granting pre-emptive rights for all miners, congressional debates showed little support for that doctrine. Many congressmen continued to believe that the mineral lands would bring rich returns to the public treasury if they went on the auction block. Apparently these men had forgotten the disappointing financial result of the sale in Missouri. Again, to admit a need for pre-emption ran counter to a strong argument in favor of sale. The case for pre-emption was the need to protect men who had settled the land and invested in improving it. But the case for sale was that men would not invest in land until they owned it. Given this dilemma, it is perhaps not surprising that only one senator, Michigan's Lyon, spoke out clearly in favor of pre-emption.

While congressmen debated the value of the lead lands and Wisconsin's territorial legislature dispatched memorials to Washington urging sale with pre-emptive rights, two cases contesting the power of the federal government to own mineral lands for an extended period of time moved slowly through the courts.

The first case involved J. P. B. Gratiot, who in 1834 obtained a smelting license from Thomas Legate, Superintendent of the Lead Mines. Gratiot executed a bond signed by two bondsmen, guaranteeing to pay to the United States six pounds of lead for every one hundred pounds smelted from federal mines. In 1836 the United States brought suit to recover upon this promise, alleging that Gratiot had smelted 2,400 pounds of lead, but had steadfastly refused to pay the rent. Gratiot and the bondsmen denied that the President or his appointed representative had power to issue a smelting license, and when the lower court was evenly divided on this issue, the question was certified to the United States Supreme Court.

The colorful and indefatigable senator from Missouri, Thomas Hart Benton, appeared to contest the case against Attorney General Gilpin, representing the United States. Mr. Benton rested his case upon an interpretation of the Fourth Article of the United States Constitution which provides: "Congress shall have the power to dispose of and make all needful rules and regulations respecting the territory or other property belonging to the United States." Benton construed this language by emphasizing the words "power to dispose of," and he argued that Congress could pass no valid law retaining ownership of United States territory. He denied that there existed any federal power to engage in "the broad business of leasing public lands." The words in the Fourth Article granting Congress power to "make all needful rules and regulations respecting the territory . . . belonging to the United States," Benton construed to mean all rules and regulations looking toward immediate sale, not rules designed to preserve and manage federal property for long periods of time. Benton's strict construction of the Constitution was colored by his own dislike of the leasing system. Had he been successful in his argument, the nation's history would have been materially altered. Benton's argument denied Congress power to provide national parks and forests without a constitutional amendment.

The Supreme Court unanimously rejected the senator's argument.[25] The Court held that the Fourth Article of the Constitution granted power to Congress to retain ownership of mineral lands and to lease them for development.

The second case grew out of the fact that in 1827, Hezekiah H. Gear squatted upon federal land in the northwestern corner of Illinois with full knowledge that the tract contained a lead mine. From the time he settled there until his case was decided, he cultivated the land and occasionally dug lead ore from the earth without permission from the United States. The United States brought two suits in the Circuit Court of the United States against Gear. In one, the government sought damages for trespass upon its land, and in the other, it asked an injunction to prevent Gear from future activity which would waste federal assets. As in the *Gratiot* case, the circuit court, evenly divided and unable to decide the issues, certified a series of questions to the United States Supreme Court:

1. Did the act of June 26, 1834, which opened Wisconsin land for sale, repeal the lead land reservation contained in the 1807 law?

2. Did the act of June 26, 1834, order the President to sell the lead lands or did it merely give him the power to open them if he thought best?

3. Was there any law of Congress which authorized pre-emption in favor of a settler upon lead lands?

4. Was digging lead ore on federal land the type of act which entitled the United States to an injunction to prevent waste?

Attorney General Nelson, representing the United States, argued that Congress never intended to include the lead lands in any law authorizing federal land sales. He maintained that the 1807 reservation was unaffected by any law subsequently passed and that there existed no legal right for any person to claim pre-emption to lead lands. To prove congressional intent, the Attorney General pointed to many federal laws passed after 1807 specifically exempting reserved lead lands from pre-emption.

As his Supreme Court counsel, Gear chose Representative Hardin of Illinois, a man from the West who had long fought the federal reservation and leasing system. Counsel Hardin based his argument upon the point that the 1807 law reserved the lead lands from sale only until later disposition by Congress. He urged that the 1834 law ordered the lands sold, thus ending the 1807 reservation. He contended that Congress intended the 1834 law to dispose of the lead lands because the act did not specifically exempt them from sale. The 1834 act did specifically exclude from sale military post lands, section sixteen in each township, and other designated lands, but was silent about continued reservation of mineral lands. Hardin further argued that the 1834 act ordered the lead lands sold, and that thereafter the pre-emption laws applied to them.

Five justices of the United States Supreme Court, a majority, held that the 1807 reservation was unaffected by the 1834 act, that the 1834 act granted discretionary power to the President to sell the lead lands, that for lead lands there existed no legal right to pre-emption, and that the United States was entitled to the requested injunction against waste.[26] Three justices thought the 1834 act had repealed the 1807 reservation policy.

Although the reservation and leasing system withstood all attacks in the courts, while these two cases were progressing slowly to final decision federal officials administering the program halted their efforts. Until the cases were decided by the Supreme Court, miners refused to comply with federal law, emphasizing that in both cases the lower court was evenly divided on the legal issues. Eager for any excuse to defy federal authority, the miners profited by the long legal history of the *Gratiot* and *Gear* cases.

Bills ordering sale of the Wisconsin and Illinois lead lands failed in 1842, 1843, and 1844. General agreement could not be reached upon the minimum sale price. The War Department desired a $10 per acre minimum; individual congressmen often proposed either $5.00 or $2.50 per acre as a floor.

In 1844 Representative Hardin decided to break the deadlock over price and, indirectly, to assist his miner constituents. Hardin now informed the House that "the value of these lands . . . were greatly overrated."[27] For many years congressmen had been told by their western colleagues that the mineral lands were extremely valuable.

The Owen Report, memorials from the Wisconsin Territorial Legislature, and statements by members of Congress personally acquainted
with the area all spoke in glowing terms of the great wealth beneath
the earth's surface. But congressmen were being told the exact opposite, by a man who also came from the area and should know the
facts. Many legislators were perplexed.

There was no way that an accurate valuation of the lands could
be made. The Owen Report made no attempt to value the lands, and
congressmen were informed that the lands could not be appraised
because there was no reliable way to determine what was below the
surface of the earth. Representative George Summers spoke the feelings of a majority of lawmakers when he complained that the House
was called upon to "pass the bill in utter ignorance of the value of
what they were going to sell." His confusion resulted because, as he
put it, "[although] the gentlemen from Illinois and Missouri had told
the House that the lands were of little value, they had been told by
other gentlemen that their value was immense." [28] By the mid-1840's
Wisconsin and Illinois miners and their representatives in Washington so desperately wanted the land sold that they, like Benton and
the Missouri miners almost twenty years earlier, were willing to
belittle the value to obtain congressional consent to the sale.

Almost before the ink was dry on the *Gear* opinion, western congressmen began forceful efforts to enact a law selling the lead lands.
Representative Hoge of Illinois proposed that the lands in Illinois,
Wisconsin, and Iowa *"supposed* to contain lead mines"[29] be ordered
sold with no minimum price stated. [Italics added.] Eastern lawmakers, led by Mr. Rathbun of New York, proposed an amendment
establishing a minimum price, first at $10 per acre, and when that
was defeated, at $5 per acre. Representative McClernand of Illinois
accused the New Yorker of seeking a high minimum price so that
ordinary settlers could not afford to buy the land, with the result
that only eastern speculators would be able to purchase.

It appears to be his disposition to favor the acquisition of lands by speculators . . . , even at the expense of meritorious settlers. . . . He seems to
prefer speculators, and large profits, to the sale of the lands at a less price

to the poor, who would live upon them, cultivate them, and thus add to the general wealth, and to the virtue, honesty, and dignity of the American character.

McClernand next discoursed upon the value of the lands.

An egregious error has prevailed in regard to the value of these lands, and the general unacquaintance of the public with their value for many years; and this has been the cause of the long-standing controversy which has been kept up in and out of Congress about them. . . . They are not . . . worth as much as an equal quantity . . . as could be designated in Illinois, fit only for agricultural purposes.

Warming to his task, McClernand borrowed arguments formulated by Senator Benton many years earlier. The 1807 reservation "violated the resolution of 1785, . . . and the ordinance of 1787." His view was that the eastern states had surrendered their western land claims upon the understanding and pledge that the central government would dispose of the land and that the national government had broken this agreement. If this argument failed he had still another:

What constitutional authority has the Government to make itself a permanent general land owner? What right has it to hold lands except to dispose of them for purposes of settlement and cultivation? . . . What right has it to do any of those things any more than to embark in foreign and domestic trade, or in manufacture, or any other private enterprise or business?
. . . Tenancy may be an appropriate feature of aristocracy, but cheap lands are the bulwark of republicanism.[30]

His parting argument was the most scholarly, if not the most convincing, of all. Limited land ownership by a few, he concluded, brought about the battles of Pharsalia and Philippi and the overthrow of the Roman Republic. He left the subject there, that his colleagues might ponder whether they desired such a fate for the young republic which they were striving to perfect.

Answering this attack, Mr. Rathbun professed his interest in selling the lands, but thought congressmen should worry about securing a true value in exchange. He withdrew his amendment establishing a minimum price of $5 per acre, and the bill passed the House.

The Senate abandoned its own bill authorizing sale and passed the House bill. On July 11, 1846, President Polk signed the bill into law.[31]

The act provided that lead land sales should be conducted in the same manner as sales of other federal lands with the following exceptions:

1. The President should cause six months' notice to be given of the sales; the notice should state facts pertaining to the number and location of mines, the probabilities of finding further ore in the area, the facilities for manufacturing products from the ore and the transportation possibilities.

2. No pre-emption should be granted until after the lands had been offered for public sale.

3. No lands should be sold upon which there was a lease in existence.

4. The lands should be sold in such subdivisions as would include any mine then being worked.

5. No bid should be received at the public sale, nor for one year thereafter, for less than $2.50 per acre.

6. After one year had elapsed, the mineral lands should be subject to sale on the same terms as other federal lands—which meant at $1.25 per acre. By Presidential proclamation, May 24, 1847, was set as the date to sell the mineral lands.

Had the bill lacked provisions to secure some premium price for the lands, passage would have been doubtful. By establishing a minimum price of $2.50 per acre for a one-year period, the law satisfied many congressmen and did not harm the miners. Resourceful to the end, they banded together in "voluntary" associations to guarantee that members would secure their lands at $1.25 per acre. These associations ruthlessly coerced mineral-lands claimants to become members, and just as ruthlessly controlled the bidding at the auctions by making things uncomfortable for any speculator who had the courage to bid at the public sale. The result was that out of 96,495.25 acres of mineral lands sold in Wisconsin, only 1,580.14 acres brought more than $2.00 per acre; the rest sold for the $1.25 minimum price applicable to other federal lands.[32]

The sale law met with general approval in the Wisconsin Territorial Legislature. Only minor objections were contained in memorials to Washington after the law was enacted. The sale law provided that no land upon which a federal lease was outstanding should be sold until the lease expired or was extinguished. Accordingly the Presidential proclamation excluded such lands, and they were not sold in 1847. In 1848 the territorial legislature memorialized President Polk to authorize sale of these lands because, the memorial alleged, the development of the area could not proceed until they were privately owned. It is somewhat ironic that miners who took leases or permits from the federal government found themselves penalized by having their lands withheld from sale for an additional period.

During the years that the reservation and leasing policy was followed many patents were withheld from purchasers because the public or private sales were alleged to have been accompanied by irregularities or fraud. To clear these cases Congress granted authority to the Commissioner of the General Land Office to determine whether or not patents should be issued in these cases. He was directed to base his decision upon "principles of equity and justice, as recognized in the courts of equity." [33] Out of 566 cases where the patent had been withheld, only 18 sales were invalidated for fraud or irregularity. The cases were judged mainly upon affidavits of the party in possession that he knew nothing wrong about the means used to secure the sale certificate from the government. Such a procedure was not designed to probe deeply the procedures under which the lands were sold. By 1847 most of the lands had been sold two or three times over, and it would have been unusual for the person in possession in 1847 to know anything about the manner in which the first buyer secured the certificate of sale from the land office. Thus vendees were protected where they could show that they were not parties to the wrongdoing and where they had paid hard-earned dollars for what they supposed their vendor had a perfect right to sell.

The success or failure of the forty years of government ownership of the lead mines of Missouri, Iowa, Wisconsin, and Illinois should be discussed only with reference to the objectives sought by the advocates of the policy. If government profit was desired, this objective was not even approximated. However, there is little evidence to suggest that enriching the federal treasury played any large role in the thinking of congressmen until about 1820, and then the objective was put forward as a straw man by the opponents of the federal program, who later destroyed it by a balancing-of-the-books argument.

There is evidence to suggest that the leasing policy was inaugurated to prevent a monopolistic development of a limited natural resource. No monopoly in lead arose, although Moses M. Strong and his associates made unsuccessful moves to establish one. Had Strong's plan succeeded, it might have been said that the federal policy of reservation aided rather than hindered the creation of a monopoly. But the plan failed. Admittedly, other forces were at work which widely dispersed ownership of the lead lands, not the least of these being a large and vocal group of ruggedly individual miners who had invested too much time and labor in their plots to stand idly by and allow ownership of substantial blocks of lead lands to become concentrated in the hands of a few persons.

Another initial objective of the 1807 policy, governmental control of a resource of war, is easily lost sight of because good fortune made it unnecessary for the United States to engage in any large military operation prior to the date when the lands were sold. The validity of the idea that lead should be reserved in the interests of national defense was never tested. Had the nation found need for vast amounts of lead, the federal policy would have facilitated a managed production and controlled use of lead through ownership of the producing mines.

The leasing system may have induced some wasteful mining practices by encouraging miners to extract the easily secured ores and then move to other locations before ores which were more expensive to mine were reached. But the same practice would have prevailed had the titles been owned by private absentee owners. Conservation of the lead mines was ignored more because such an idea was foreign to the people than because the owner was the federal government. Rapid exploitation of natural resources was the goal rather than careful husbanding of resources as a hedge against future shortage.

There certainly was an element of government ownership in the lead mines, since the United States held the title. But development proceeded under concepts of private property and individual enterprise, for the holders of the leases or permits were private individuals motivated by the profit they could make over and above the government rent. After the United States sold the lead lands, all aspects of government ownership terminated and the lands, along with other mineral resources, passed almost exclusively into the ambit of state control.

3

Industrial Ingredients: Land

THE TERMS GOVERNING access to land and its mineral wealth provided the basic legal framework within which exploitation of Wisconsin's mineral resources proceeded. Legal policy was here inextricably involved with the process of economic development, because government—the United States, or the state as its grantee—originally owned all the land. Thus, any decisions taken in law affected this area of the economy, whatever philosophy prevailed concerning government's role in relation to private ventures.

In handling the mineral lands, three main options were opened to the United States (and to the state, so far as it succeeded to the federal title): (1) government might retain the fee and restrict access to the lands, issuing only limited licenses or making particular contracts for their exploitation with government filling the role of owner-entrepreneur; (2) government might retain the fee and play the part simply of landlord, leasing the land on terms which would leave more or less entrepreneurial discretion to the lessees as to the manner and course of exploitation; (3) government might sell all or part of the fee, thus turning over completely to non-official decision-makers the initiative in determining at what speed and how the mineral wealth should be used.

Between the early nineteenth century and mid-twentieth century, federal or state public policy at one time or another pursued each of these courses in some measure. There was no neat logic about the

55

succession of policies, however. The first effort was an attempt to carry out a program of federal leases. Because this undertaking provided the first legal framework within which Wisconsin mining went on, it was necessary to explore in Chapter 2 the creation and collapse of the federal leasing program. The values and attitudes which prevailed among political leaders, the mining community, and the general public, as reflected in the course of the leasing experiment, are helpful also in understanding the frame of reference within which alternative public policies developed.

The present chapter will deal at the outset with the other two main types of disposition of the public mineral lands. The first of these was the policy of outright sale of the fee, which, at least as a *de facto* policy, accompanied the leasing program to some extent and then took over the field entirely through the second half of the nineteenth century after federal leasing was abandoned. The alternative policy —reservation and closely controlled licensing of access—did not come seriously into play until the early twentieth century, and then wholly as a program of the state, since by then there existed no substantial federal ownership of mineral land in Wisconsin. After these policies the chapter will consider an important auxiliary program which of necessity accompanied public ownership of mineral lands so long as substantial areas remain in government hands. This was the protection of public mineral lands against trespass. Finally, this chapter will examine the relation of the legal order to a system of strictly private ownership of mineral wealth.

There was little opportunity afforded Wisconsin's official decision-makers to determine the scope and terms of private mineral-land ownership. In the lead region the state was never a conduit of title. Title passed directly from the federal government to private owners before statehood. After statehood, the federal government patented thousands of other acres of Wisconsin land to private owners without special consultation with state officials beyond the views the state's congressional delegation could voice in Congress. Federal agents sold mineral lands to private owners at auction and at private sales. Homesteaders received patents from Washington directly.

Grantees of land given to finance internal public improvements received title from the federal government in many cases without the
state appearing in the chain of title. Grants to military personnel ran
directly from the federal government to the individual. In all of these
instances state control of private mineral-lands ownership was eliminated insofar as control might have been founded upon the power
of an owner to retain title or impose conditions upon a grantee.

The failure of the federal leasing program left a legacy of public
opinion adverse to all forms of government ownership of mineral
land, an attitude that lasted for many years. Federal policy affecting
Wisconsin mineral-land ownership for the rest of the nineteenth
century was not different from its policy toward all land. The existence of such a policy is not surprising in view of the difficulty of
identifying and segregating mineral-bearing acres. On the state level
failure of the federal leasing program fostered a climate which made
trouble for any leader who proposed programs of government control and ownership, or laws regulating private ownership.

Proposals to dilute the concept of private mineral-land ownership
ran also into a very strong frontier distrust of governmental control
and a desire to exploit the natural resources of the West as rapidly
as possible. In view of these strong public feelings on the subject,
it is somewhat surprising, then, that shortly after Wisconsin became
a state there were serious moves to limit private mineral-land ownership.

From about 1838 to 1848 an area of New York state near Albany
rocked with disputes between the heirs of Stephen Van Rensselaer
and hundreds of tenants occupying lands owned by the Van Rensselaer family. The tenants' initial complaint was directed against a
serious attempt by the heirs to collect $400,000 back rent. Gradually
their grievances were broadened to include a general objection to the
fact that large land areas were controlled by a small number of people. The National Reform Association grew out of this New York
conflict. By 1848 the association had leaders in Wisconsin.

In Wisconsin the association broadened its platform to include
limitation of land ownership, establishment of maximum hours for

labor, prevention of speculation in public lands, and enactment of laws to place certain property of a debtor beyond his creditors' reach. Of all of these objectives, the association most earnestly sought to achieve legal limits upon the amount of land an individual or a corporation might own.

The decade prior to 1850 demonstrated that the platform of the National Reform Association did not have sufficient popular appeal to nourish a new political party, even when espoused by such a national figure as Horace Greeley. Accordingly, association leaders in Wisconsin decided to operate within existing party lines. They sought to secure from regular party members a pledge in favor of the association's programs. Such Wisconsin political figures as James Doty, Moses M. Strong, Charles Dunn, and James Cross were pledged to the principles of the association.

Upon three separate occasions proposals were presented to the Wisconsin legislature to limit land holdings in Wisconsin, including the holding of mineral lands. The first two occasions were not serious. In 1848 some "Rock County citizens" petitioned the legislature to limit land ownership. Although the petition brought forth a committee report sympathetic to the idea, formal floor action was postponed by the plea that the end of the session was too near to work out the plan. The report stated: "It is the duty of government to secure all her people in possession of sufficient land for their wants, and to prevent an undue monopoly of it by any." [1]

In 1849 a citizen, Beriah Brown, petitioned the legislature for a law limiting land ownership. He touched off a political feud between the majority and minority of a legislative committee. The majority advised Brown to join the "free demoncratic party," and the minority retorted that Brown had "discretion" enough to pick his own party. [2]

After the 1850 session of the state legislature, the National Reform Association speeded up its activities in a serious effort to obtain a law limiting land ownership. In his 1851 annual message Governor Dewey skirted the issue by leaving it to the legislature. His uncertainty about the political implications of the issue led him to leave his own views unclear. About a week later, a select committee reported a bill which prohibited individual ownership of more than 320 acres or more than two city lots of 1 acre each. The bill banned future purchases in excess of these limits, and provided that all acreage purchased above that figure should escheat to the state. Other provisions reduced existing estates to the legal size upon the death of the owner.

Quickly sensing that legislative votes were about evenly divided, opponents counterattacked. Many newspapers and speakers argued that the law would put an end to private enterprise and destroy incentive, that its provision for paying a fee to informers would divide communities and disrupt society, and, in a more legalistic argument, that the law was unconstitutional. The proponents held mass meetings against monopoly, land speculation, long hours for labor, and absentee ownership. A chairman of one giant Milwaukee meeting, attended by over a thousand people, ruled out of order a resolution that read: *"Resolved:* That all property in the United States, the State of Wisconsin, and the city of Milwaukee, ought to be divided every Saturday night, and oftener if necessary." [3]

When support for the bill dwindled, its sponsors doubled the maximum acre figures. The death of the bill was hastened by an opinion of the attorney general of Wisconsin which declared that the measure would be unconstitutional. Considering the prevailing climate of opinion, the final vote defeating the bill was close: 39 to 27.

From the date of this defeat to the middle of the twentieth century, the legal history of the state is almost barren of any direct interference with the concept of private property in mineral lands. World War I prompted the Wisconsin legislature to urge the national government in 1917 to "[take over] all mines and oil fields and their wells without profit under the federal bureau of mines." [4] And in 1923 the state urged federal legislation to "secure government ownership and operation of all coal mines." [5] In the twentieth century Wisconsin operated a granite quarry to assist in constructing state buildings. [6] Local government subdivisions owned and operated gravel pits, but they did so only to produce supplies for consumption by governmental consumers, and not for resale to individuals for profit. [7] Apart from these minor activities, the state was willing to allow persons who purchased mineral lands to own them as they would farm, grazing, or timber lands.

As previously pointed out, ownership of hundreds of thousands of acres of Wisconsin land went directly from the federal government to individuals and corporations. However, many thousands, and even millions, of other acres passed through the hands of the state or units of local government. Included in the latter category were the swampland patents, the school and university grants, and in some cases grants to aid works of internal improvements. With respect to these an easy opportunity was presented the state government to alter or control the private ownership of mineral wealth.

Arguments in favor of governmental ownership of mineral wealth rested upon a solid logical base. The value of mineral land resulted largely from fortuitous factors. Human beings played no role in placing the ore in particular places. Since human effort was far less responsible for the large returns from mineral land than for those from agricultural land, men had less claim to riches of mineral land. Admittedly, contrary arguments existed, but the policy of government ownership of mineral wealth in non-dictatorial countries in Europe rested upon this basic argument.

The twentieth century witnessed little use of potential state power in this area. Two separate movements gave evidence that the state government realized the existence of important social benefits which could be secured by state control of state-owned land. Of course, by the dawn of the twentieth century, most state-owned land had been sold, and the opportunity to make large-scale alteration of the institution of private ownership of mineral land had disappeared.

In 1903 the legislature decreed that thenceforth no person might buy more than 160 acres of state land.[8] The law required each buyer to affirm by affidavit that he did not hold more than 160 acres of state land purchased after October 15, 1903. To prevent a dummy from purchasing land and then conveying it to another person, the law further required each buyer to affirm that he had no agreement or understanding that he would convey the state land to any person or corporation in the future. In 1917 the legislature changed the terms of the affidavit to require the buyer to swear that his holdings "heretofore purchased" did not exceed 160 acres.[9]

These restrictions prevailed until 1951. Their repeal was effected by an omnibus bill whose title declared its purpose to be the abolition of "obsolete and unworkable" laws.[10] Speculation suggests that the law was unworkable because affidavits would not prevent evasion, and that it was obsolete because by 1951 few acres of state land remained, and practically none were for sale.

The acreage restriction enacted in 1903 coincided with other efforts to conserve the state's natural resources, mineral as well as timber. The timing indicates that the restrictions were motivated by a conservation theory, rather than by conscious effort to change private mineral ownership as such. A second policy suggestion approached the conservation objective in more direct fashion.

From the date the federal government sold the lead lands until 1909, the legal history of mineral lands parallels the legal history of agricultural lands. But in 1909 the state legislature decreed:

> Whenever the state of Wisconsin shall hereafter convey . . . any of its land, the conveyance thereof shall be subject to the continuous ownership by the state of all minerals in said lands, and all mining rights therein. . . . Such conveyance shall also be subject to a continuing easement in the state . . . to enter and occupy such lands in any manner necessary and convenient to the removal of such minerals from such lands and to the proper exercise of such mineral rights.[11]

Although the legislature repealed this stipulation in 1913, the policy was continued by a 1911 enactment which applied an identical reservation to "every contract, certificate of sale, or grant . . . of public lands." [12] This policy was similar, but not exactly analogous, to the federal reservation of lead lands. The important difference was that the state reserved only the underlying mineral wealth, and not the title to both surface and subsurface areas. Farmers, lumber companies, or any other users might purchase surface rights, but any and all subterranean minerals remained state property. The only disadvantage the surface owner might suffer in the use of his surface property would occur when the state used the reserved surface easement to remove the minerals.

The legal technique of dividing land ownership horizontally, of putting one owner in almost complete enjoyment of the surface and another in control of the subsurface minerals, was a late arrival as applied to governmental lands. Long before 1900 private owners had often divided land ownership in this manner, but the federal and state governments had not used the technique. In the 1830's many settlers desired to purchase federal land which the law reserved as lead bearing. Of these settlers, many contemplated farming rather than mining. It would have abated much local criticism, had the federal government sold surface estates, reserving only the minerals.

From 1909 to 1917 Wisconsin lawmakers made no provision for working or leasing the reserved minerals on state-owned lands. By 1917 jurisdiction over state lands was divided between two state agencies: the Commissioners of Public Lands and the Conservation Commission. The latter exercised authority over state parks and state forests; the former over all other state lands. In 1917 both agencies obtained power to grant "licenses . . . to prospect for ore or mineral" on land under their respective jurisdictions.[13] This limited power to grant permits "to prospect" was extended in 1925, for lands governed by Public Lands Commissioners, to include licenses to "prospect for and to dig and remove . . . ore, minerals and other deposits . . . for a full and fair consideration paid to the state, the amount and terms whereof shall be fixed by said commission."[14] The power of the Conservation Commission was not likewise extended.

In 1911 proponents of state ownership of mineral wealth sought to embody in the state constitution not only the policy of the above-mentioned 1909 and 1911 legislation reserving mineral rights to the state on all property sold by the state, but also a sweeping limitation of private property rights. As originally worded the proposed constitutional amendment would have (1) prohibited sale or disposal of all existing or future-acquired state minerals, (2) prohibited the leasing of state mineral lands to private persons for profit, and (3) adopted the following novel provision: "All mineral rights hitherto reserved in contracts, deeds, or instruments conveying real estate are abolished and shall be inoperative after January 1, 1920 and are declared to inhere in the state except where such mineral rights have been developed in whole or in part previous to January 1, 1920." [15] Owners of private mineral rights taken by the state under the provision were to be compensated for their property.

For many years, grantors of Wisconsin land had commonly reserved for themselves the mineral estate when they conveyed land. The practice had become customary, whether or not there existed any basis for belief that the land contained minerals. Success of the proposed constitutional changes would have brought to the state a vast number of these reserved estates. The valuation problems involved in such a change would have been great.

The motive behind the proposal remains obscure. Probably more than one reason existed. By 1911 conservation interest was running high. There is also evidence that many land titles were clouded by mineral reservations, and the proposed change may have been designed to eliminate the undeveloped mineral reservations from these titles.

A senate committee quickly struck out the words in the proposed amendment which swept into state ownership the mineral estates in thousands of acres of privately owned land. The committee approved the reservation of all mineral rights in state lands and a provision that these rights should never be alienated. It approved also the leasing of state-owned mineral estates when authorized by the vote of two-thirds of the total membership of each legislative house. As thus amended, the proposition passed both houses.

The Wisconsin constitution required that two successive legislatures approve a proposed amendment before it could be put to popular vote. In 1913 the legislature changed some language in the amendment unrelated to the reservation of mineral estates. The proposal was then laid before the next legislature in 1915. That body refused approval and the amendment was never submitted to the electorate. However, the several statutes discussed above remained law throughout the first half of the twentieth century.

A plethora of problems accompanied state ownership of hundreds of thousands of acres of land. Vexing policy and administrative questions surrounded the sale of this land. But no issue proved as troublesome as protecting the vast state holdings from trespassers. Trespassers on timber land outnumbered trespassers on mineral land a hundredfold, for more state land possessed virgin timber than minerals, and timber thieving was less easily detected than mineral thieving. But mineral trespassers on both state and private lands were a menace the state sought for years to control by law, often by legislation designed to apply to timber thieves and mineral trespassers alike.

The exact amount of mineral trespassing cannot be estimated. No figures recording the toll taken by human predators appeared in any Wisconsin public document. Many trespassers existed, though, particularly in the lead region where we are told the jumping of claims made the legal machinery hum.[16] The considerable number of mineral trespassing cases in the Wisconsin Supreme Court are evidence of the fact that mineral trespassers operated widely, although they were not as serious a problem as timber thieves.

In their efforts to control trespassing, lawmakers placed greatest emphasis upon the criminal law, the historic regulator of activities harmful to society as a whole. From 1844 until 1887, mineral trespassing was branded criminal by territorial or state statutes separate from the ordinary criminal code provisions on offenses against property rights. An 1844 statute declared a misdemeanor the unauthorized digging of mineral upon school or university lands. Punishment included a maximum of a year's confinement in the county jail or a fine between $5 and $500.

Throughout the years changes were made in the punishment for mineral trespassing. In 1849, for example, the legislature added a three-month minimum sentence but deleted the minimum fine. In 1865 the legislature set maximum penalties of six months' imprisonment and a fine of $1,000. By 1893 anyone who "[took or carried away] any mineral, earth or stone" was penalized by not more than six months in jail or a fine of not over $100.

The special treatment accorded mineral trespassers prior to 1887 is evident from the fact that in 1887 the legislature established more severe penalties for the act of taking away with intent to steal "anything which is parcel of the reality or annexed thereto." This wrongful conduct the legislature labeled "larceny," as distinguished from the less serious "misdemeanor" applicable to mineral trespassers upon public lands. Punishment for larceny varied from one to five years in the state prison if the property stolen was over $100 in value, to six months in the county jail if the property was under $20 in value.

After 1893 mineral trespassers were generally regulated by the criminal code on the same terms as persons who stole any other type of personal property; no separate criminal code provision remained applicable to their actions. For example, under both the 1951 Wisconsin Revised Statutes and the 1953 revised criminal code, mineral trespassers were not given separate treatment, and the punishment varied according to the value of the property stolen.

One may doubt what value the criminal code had in regulating mineral trespassers in the nineteenth century. Through the history of the state not one criminal case involving a mineral trespass ever resulted in an opinion by the Wisconsin Supreme Court. Any extensive use of the criminal law would certainly have produced one appellate opinion. Nor is there any evidence that increased penalties had material consequences.

The failure of the criminal law to control mineral trespass was attributable most directly to the slight public opprobrium accorded the activity. For most of the nineteenth century, Wisconsin's lawmakers made the crime only a misdemeanor; local policemen and sheriffs, sensitive to local views, did not look hard for violators, or looked the other way. Elected district attorneys failed or refused to prosecute; juries drawn from the offender's neighborhood would not return indictments or convict. Without attempting to change the jury system, whose historic roots rendered it impregnable, nine-teenth-century legislators experimented, often half-heartedly, with legal techniques designed to circumvent the public apathy and hostility which made the criminal law impotent against trespass on state lands.

The fact that state land holdings were far flung and extensive had always made it difficult to catch and convict trespassers. By an 1849 law the legislature informed local school superintendents that it was their "special duty" to report to the district attorney all tres-passers coming to their attention.[17] In 1865 the legislature placed this duty upon the Commissioners of School and University Lands.[18] The same legislature sought to recruit informers by authorizing payment of up to 25 per cent of a trespasser's fine to anyone who gave information about or testified against the wrongdoer.[19]

In the above-mentioned 1849 law the legislature specially ordered the district attorney to prosecute trespassers on state lands, and the 1865 law authorized payments of up to 10 per cent of the fine recovered to district attorneys who prosecuted trespassers success-fully. Finally, in 1905 the legislature condemned trespassers on state lands and stipulated:

> Whenever an arrest shall have been made for any violation of any provision of this act, or whenever any information shall have been lodged with him, it shall be the duty of the district attorney of the county in which the criminal act was committed to prosecute the offender or of-fenders. If any district attorney shall fail to comply with the provisions of this section, he shall be guilty of a misdemeanor and upon conviction shall be fined not less than $100 nor more than $1,000, or be imprisoned not less than thirty days nor more than one year or both in the discretion of the court. The penalties of this section shall apply to any magistrate, with proper authority, who refuses or neglects without cause to issue a warrant for the arrest and prosecution of any person or persons when complaint, under oath, of violation of any of the terms of this act has been lodged with him.[20]

To make the prosecutor's task simpler, a statute provided that a certificate from the secretary of state would be prima facie evidence that the state owned the land upon which the trespass occurred.

Desperate over failure of regular officials to detect violations, the state in 1860 provided four special clerks to protect state lands. For the rest of the century a number of these special state employees cruised the northern reaches of the state seeking to discover and apprehend violators. In 1864 the number was eight; in 1865 the legislature left the number discretionary with the Commissioners of School and University Lands within certain budget limits; in 1871 the number was four; in 1876, eight; and in 1891 the number was again made subject to the commissioners' discretion. From 1891 on until well into the twentieth century, the number varied in the discretion of various state officials and boards, including the clerk of the Commissioners of Public Lands, the state forester, and the Conservation Commission. Throughout the years the special officers were called various names: clerks, agents, and woodsmen.

Meager appropriations for these agents often hampered their work. In 1860 the total of the four salaries could not exceed $2,000; in 1864, $4,000. In 1871, $6,000 was appropriated to cover salaries and expenses. Five dollar per diem payments, plus expenses, compensated them in 1891, but a ceiling of $4,000 per year destroyed needed flexibility. In 1871 and again in 1905 the legislatures authorized special pay for the trespass agents from fines recovered:

Nothing herein or in law of this state shall prevent the . . . commissioners . . . [of public lands] from paying said clerks by allowing them a percentage upon the moneys received from the sale of material seized, and from payments of penalties on account of such trespasses.[21]

The state forester is authorized to approve for payment to any trespass agent . . . upon whose evidence successful action is brought for trespass . . . not to exceed 25 per centum of the amount collected for such trespass . . . provided that in no case shall such payment exceed five hundred dollars ($500.00).[22]

To aid these agents in the proper performance of their duties, the legislature in 1865 declared guilty of a misdemeanor one who (1) knowingly obstructed a trespass agent in the performance of his duties or (2) procured or counseled anyone to do so or (3) willfully removed or caused to be removed from the possession of the agent, materials seized in the discharge of his duties. An oath of office for the agents and a ban on their dealing in state lands represented other attempts to strengthen their performance.

On the debit side, however, in 1876 the appointing power was transferred from the Commissioners of School and University Lands to the Governor, and the positions immediately became objects of political patronage seekers. There is some evidence that these officers, in spite of their handicaps, made themselves felt in the areas they surveyed. However, they were too few in number, the public indifference was too great, and the state's holdings were too large for them to protect state lands in any large measure.

While the criminal law made futile efforts to overcome a lack of public indignation against trespassers, an attitude that had built up over a long period when many settlers upon federal lands were technically trespassers, the state sought to eliminate the trespass problem by disposing of the state domain as rapidly as possible. Much land was sold on time payments: the state put the purchaser in possession with a certificate of sale as evidence of his rights until he could pay for the land and obtain the patent. To prevent a defaulting certificate holder from forfeiting to the state land stripped of its mineral wealth, laws generally denied the certificate holder the right to subtract minerals prior to the time he secured a patent. Because of a deficiency in the common law, the certificate holder probably lacked sufficient interest in the land to sue a trespasser for civil damages occasioned by a trespass during the certificate period. In 1864 whatever doubt existed under judge-made law disappeared when the legislature stipulated:

> Any person . . . holding a certificate of sale . . . shall have the same right to . . . maintain action to recover damages for injuries . . . or to prevent tresp[a]sses thereon . . . by injunctions . . . as if such person . . . [was] the owner . . . ; and . . . the holder . . . of any certificate . . . shall be regarded . . . as the real owner of the land from . . . the time of payment by him of the first installment of the payment of the purchase money.[23]

One year later the legislature conferred on all patent holders the right to (1) seize or sue for any minerals removed from the land "before the issue of . . . [the] patent . . . as if the . . . [minerals] had been . . . removed from . . . [the] land after the issue of . . . [the] patent" and (2) to bring an action for damages caused to the land by trespass committed before the patent issued "as if such trespass had been committed after the patent had issued." [24] By granting certificate and patent holders the right to bring actions against trespassers, both of these laws sought to shift to private persons the initiative and responsibility for civil enforcement of property rights in minerals.

In the fight to protect its holdings, Wisconsin as a landowner—and a very large one—had at its disposal, in addition to the power of the sovereign in the criminal law area, any civil action available to a private landowner. As in the case of the criminal law, it seems unusual that not a single Wisconsin Supreme Court opinion shows the state suing for civil relief in a mineral trespass case. Of course, the state's civil remedies were likely to encounter the same road blocks as its criminal actions—dilatory prosecution, or no prosecution at all, and hostile juries. To skirt these two difficulties, in 1893 the legislature decreed:

All actions brought to recover damages for trespass upon public lands, when the amount in controversy exceeds the sum of two hundred dollars, may be commenced in the county of Dane [the capital county], or in the county in which the trespass shall have been committed, at the option of the attorney general, and shall not be subject to any change of venue therefrom.[25]

Shifting the venue from the northern counties was an attempt to eliminate the stultifying effect of local prejudices. Two years later, in 1895, the law was amended to give the attorney general power to commence such a suit in any county of the state.[26] This change may have been made because the prior law unduly burdened the Dane County courts, or unfairly prejudiced the defendant by forcing him to stand trial in a county far distant from the northern counties where the timber and minerals existed.

Beginning in 1860 the legislature embarked upon a new policy which hamstrung the effectiveness of civil, and probably also of criminal, law. At that time the law authorized clerks to apprehend trespassers and seize any property, timber or mineral, which a trespasser had severed from state lands. The 1860 legislation provided that if the land from which the property was taken was subject to private entry, the trespasser might buy the land at the appraised price, plus an additional 25 per cent of the "whole amount paid." Upon the erstwhile trespasser's complying with these provisions, he was entitled to return of the severed property, and "any and all suits commenced to recover any damages for such . . . taking, or carrying away" were to be discontinued.[27] The same consequences followed if, contrary to law, a certificate holder took minerals from the land before he secured a patent.

From 1860 to 1949 this general policy prevailed. Under it trespassers might gain immunity from civil suits by paying a premium for the land. In 1864 the penalty was increased to 50 per cent for non-certificate-holding trespassers. By 1871 the penalty was 100 per cent for both classes of trespassers (certificate holders and non-certificate holders). It remained at this figure until the whole policy was abandoned in 1949.

Through the years the legislature placed additional penalties upon trespassers who, after they were apprehended, desired to buy the land. In 1870, in addition to the penalty, the trespasser was required to pay "all the expenses of seizure and taking care of the . . . [property] until the settlement is completed . . ." before the minerals would be released to him. In 1871 the legislature ordered that no material be released to the trespasser until he had paid all penalties and charges even though after the trespass he secured a patent. And a 1917 law made non-certificate-holding trespassers ineligible to buy any other state lands until they had paid for the land they had looted, including the penalty amount and all seizure expenses.

Although payment of the penalty freed the trespasser from civil suits for damages, whether purchasing the land and paying the penalty would arrest or prevent a criminal prosecution against him was unclear for many years. In 1891 the point was clarified when the legislature declared: "Nothing in this chapter contained, nor the payment of any penalty therein provided, shall affect the liability

of any person, whether prosecuted before or after the issuance of
. . . [the] patent, to punishment for any such trespass." [28]

Beginning with the 1847 federal disposal of the lead lands, and
throughout the rest of the nineteenth century, both state and federal
governments rapidly disposed of their Wisconsin land without separate consideration or treatment of its mineral character. Throughout
this period, and with only a small-scale return to a policy of state
ownership in the twentieth century, the ownership rights and management decisions surrounding Wisconsin mineral wealth rested
in the hands of private entrepreneurs, corporate and non-corporate.

Like the state as landowner, these private owners faced the problem of protecting their property from trespassers. The criminal code
early declared it a misdemeanor to carry away minerals from private
lands. There is no evidence that this proved an adequate protection.
No criminal cases of trespass on private lands resulted in a Wisconsin
Supreme Court opinion.

In addition to the criminal law, private mineral owners had available civil remedies devised by English common law judges centuries
before Wisconsin became a state. As the common law stood in Wisconsin in 1850, the remedies existed almost unaltered. These remedies
were not developed specifically for the protection of mineral lands,
but such lands were not so radically unlike farmlands as to make
the remedies unworkable. Law courts provided landowners with
the opportunity to sue to recover the value of the severed ore. Some
courts even entertained suits seeking return of the ore in specie.
There existed the possibility of legal actions to recover possession
of the real estate, and courts of equity would enjoin wrongdoers
from trespassing. Fines, and even jail sentences, compelled obedience
to these injunctions. In the lead-mining period, there is evidence
that miners often resorted to civil actions to protect their claims.[29]
A considerable number of civil trespass cases involving private mineral-land owners appeared before the Wisconsin Supreme Court.[30]

Through the years legislative modifications of these civil remedies
were slight. During the federal-ownership period many defendants
challenged the right of plaintiffs holding various interests in the

real estate to bring civil actions. Generally, the common law remedies specified above were available to the fee owner or someone claiming rightfully under him. But by 1835 people of diverse status claimed interests in Wisconsin lead lands; many of their claims were of types unknown to the common law. Men purchased land from the federal land office and obtained a receipt from the receiver. Until a patent was issued this receipt was the only evidence the purchasers had of their property rights. Patents were slow in arriving owing to normal slowness of communication, overworked land office personnel, and frequent disputes over claims. The common law provided no ready-made rules to apply to a person holding such an interest. In 1836 the territorial legislature provided that the land office receiver's receipt should be evidence in all territorial courts of the holder's right to federal land.[31] But in 1838 the lawmakers provided that these receipts should not be good evidence of ownership "for any lands held, owned or occupied by any person or persons as mineral ground at the time of said entry, and on which discoveries of lead or copper ore shall have been made." [32] This provision protected miners who were working a plot at the time someone entered it at the federal land office. Finally, in 1839 a law permitted a "squatter" (one who occupied federal land without any patent or receipt) to sue trespassers as if the squatter were a full owner. Miners and the small work plots they possessed were again exempted from this law.

As these illustrations show, private-property interests in minerals gave trouble to the legal order in only minor respects of doctrine. Wisconsin mineral-land owners often separated ownership of the subsurface mineral estate from ownership of the surface area. This separation was accomplished either by granting the minerals to another, or by reserving the minerals when the surface was conveyed. In either case, the practice forced the law to determine the nature of the separate ownership of the minerals for a variety of purposes. Usually the issue was whether the separate mineral owner owned real or personal property. For example, state statutes required written documents to create an interest in real estate; judgment creditors might levy on real estate; brokers had to have a license to negotiate a sale of an interest in real estate; certain legal actions could be brought only by a person having rights in real estate.

For the solution of these questions, the law determined whether a transaction between two parties gave rise to an interest in the minerals while they were in the ground, unsevered, or whether the transaction involved only permission to come upon the land (a license) to remove the minerals. In the latter case, ownership of tangible physical objects came into being only when the ore was severed and had become personal property.

In these cases the issue was a narrow one, turning almost always on the intent of the parties. Their intent was usually totally obscured rather than revealed by the language they had used; sometimes the transactions were oral and testimony conflicting. Throughout the history of territory and state, Wisconsin mineral-land owners might create either a mere license or an interest in real estate if their intent was clearly expressed. The law's concept of the nature of mineral ownership raised no real impediment to free human development of the mineral resources.

By fiat, one legislative enactment added a term to all mineral leases. This 1860 act provided that whether the lease was written or oral, if it provided nothing to the contrary, it should not be

revocable by the maker . . . , after a valuable discovery or prospect . . . [had] been struck, unless the miner . . . [should] forfeit his right by negligence, such as establishes a forfeiture according to mining usages. . . . Usages and customs among miners may be proved in explanation of mining contracts, to the same extent as usage may be proved in other branches of business.[33]

The legislature here sought to protect a miner who found ore, but whose lease did not specify a termination date. The risk the statute eliminated was a speedy revocation of the lease by the owner after the discovery. The law left untouched leases which contained an expiration date.

Judicial treatment of this statute deprived it of much meaning. The court's main handiwork consisted of defining when a miner "struck" a "valuable discovery or prospect." The Wisconsin Supreme Court characterized the origin of the law, and also hinted at its future judicial treatment:

[The law] is in many respects a very peculiar statute, and its provisions, as well as its peculiar use of mining terms, indicate a local origin. It applies only to mining contracts and leases for the digging of ores and minerals. . . . The class of contracts affected is . . . very narrow. But with regard to a contract which does fall within its provisions . . . [it is] quite sweeping.

. . . .

. . . Under such a statute the word "discovery" must in the interest of certainty of titles have a reasonably strict construction.[34]

Because of peculiar geological formations in the lead region, lead crevices, or veins, often stopped abruptly, only to be discovered a few feet or yards distant in the same general direction. Supreme court judges decided that any miner who prospected ahead of where his old crevice had "pinched out," did not meet the statutory test of having "struck" a "valuable discovery."[35] In effect, the supreme court added the adjective "new" to qualify the statute's protection of a "discovery." Other supreme court decisions did little to alter this construction, so that the statute could play only a limited role in protecting miners.

Mining customs in Wisconsin were not very important sources of mineral property rules in contrast to legal development in many western states. The 1860 "discovery" statute is an example of legislation incorporating a mining custom. Another 1860 statute incorporated the customary law by providing that a miner who failed to "work his diggings according to the usages of miners, without reasonable excuse . . . shall . . . forfeit his diggings."[36]

A 1911 Wisconsin Supreme Court opinion referred to mining custom to solve a legal dispute. A lessee took possession of mineral lands under a lease and commenced exploration, but from September 1, 1907, to November 14, 1908, did nothing. The lessor then terminated the lease and executed a lease to a second lessee, who went upon the land to explore. The first lessee then sued to enjoin the second lessee from trespassing. The supreme court held that if a lessee failed to prospect for an unreasonable length of time, the lessor was justified in forfeiting the lease even though the lease was silent upon the point. The court solved the issue of what time constituted an unreasonable delay by citing an English case which held that by the custom of Cornwall "suspension of operations by prospectors or adventurers for a year and a day was grounds for forfeiture of their interest in . . . mineral land." The court concluded: "In this age and country of greater hurry and activity the limit of suspension of prospecting should without sufficient excuse certainly not exceed that. The finding of the learned circuit court, whose circuit includes the most ancient and active mining district in this state, also supports the conclusion that the delay in the instant case was unreasonable." [37]

On the whole, Wisconsin mineral-property owners were adequately served by unmodified legal concepts and methods of adjusting property disputes that were in existence many years before any lead was removed from Wisconsin soil. However, one physical fact of mining life demanded novel use of an ancient legal tool. Particularly in the lead region many ore crevices abruptly pitched downward and encountered water. Abandonment of the location followed unless the owner could dispose of his water by pumping or by constructing an adit. Either course often required that the drainage water cross lands belonging to another. The common law provided only one method for the mine owner to effect this: he must obtain consent of the adjoining owner. If the adjoining owner was adamant or the asking price too high, a legal remedy was generally lacking.

By chapter 359, Wisconsin Laws, 1860, the state legislature provided that the mine owner might pay a reasonable price for the privelege and force a right-of-way for his waste water. The act applied to all mines and to the construction of "pipes, ditches, water races, or tunnels." Applications were made to the county judge; three disinterested commissioners determined the price of the privilege. The statute did not require any finding that the right-of-way was "necessary" or for a "public purpose," though such determinations were usual requirements for valid exercise of the sovereign power of eminent domain.

In 1878 the statutory revisors added a requirement that before granting the mine owner relief, the county judge should find that the right-of-way was "necessary for the proposed use of . . . [the] lands." The revisors' comments show that they doubted the constitutionality of the 1860 law:

Ch. 359, 1860, has appeared to the revisors to be of doubtful constitutionality. But as the question arising on it presents some aspects different from a kindred question in respect to private roads, the law for which the Supreme Court has held unconstitutional, it has seemed best to retain the provisions, especially as they relate to important interests. The provisions of the act have been condensed and amended to secure fair hearing of the parties by briefly conforming them to the principal features of the condemnation provisions in the general railroad law.[38]

The 1860 act remained in effect after 1880, but in 1880 the legislature passed a second condemnation law which furnished mine owners an alternative procedure to compel right-of-way grants. The newer enactment required that the mine owner allege that the right-of-way would "benefit . . . the public" and was "necessary for drainage of the . . . mines." A jury of twelve, replacing the three commissioners, determined the amount of compensation, after finding that it was "necessary to use such land in the construction of . . . [the] ditch" and that "the construction [would] . . . tend to the benefit or the advantage . . . [of] the public." [39]

In addition to these general drainage right-of-way statutes, special mining corporate charters in the 1850's and the 1860's contained analogous grants of eminent domain power to facilitate drainage. These charters employed various methods to determine the compensation due the adjoining land owner—by town supervisors, by a jury summoned by a justice of the peace, or by a board of three appraisers (one chosen by each party, and the third by these two).

Mine drainage brought another legal property issue which was never thought through to a policy decision, probably because of lack of sufficiently urgent demand for a solution. Frequently, one mine owner in draining his own lands unwittingly conferred a benefit upon an adjoining mineral-land proprietor by lowering the water table of all lands in the neighborhood. The first state geologist perceived the problem and hinted that the adjoining land owner who was thus benefited should be under a legal duty to pay a share of the cost.[40]

There is evidence that many of these situations were compromised by private cost-sharing agreements. The law, of course, enforced such agreements to the same extent as any other lawful contract.[41] In a unique provision, one special mining charter provided that no one should dig lead ore from ground drained by the corporation without paying reasonable charges as agreed upon by the parties, which "shall in no case exceed the one-fifth part of all minerals . . . [dug] by such person or persons, unless there be a written contract to the contrary." [42]

4

Industrial Ingredients: Capital

SCARCITY OF CAPITAL headed the list of the most vexing and obstinate problems affecting the mineral industry of Wisconsin. From territorial days (which roughly coincided with the boom period of the lead region) to the halfway point of the twentieth century, mineral promoters, honest and dishonest, sought ways and means to compete for capital. Through the lead and zinc periods, the oil boom of 1865, the Penokee orgy, several spurts of activity in copper, and finally a low-grade iron ore development, mining promoters competed with farmers, industrialists, transportation companies, and small businessmen for the favor of creditors and investors. Mining men used the legal order directly to aid in this competition in many ways—ways which form the subject of this chapter.

Lead miners who came to the Wisconsin scene before 1850 were not rich Yankee traders. They were hard-working southerners, usually Missouri miners, who brought with them no great private fortunes. As early as 1837, a writer fully familiar with the lead area summed up their problems: "Want of machinery, want of proper opening of mines, and above all, want of capital, have been great drawbacks on the prosperity of the Wisconsin lead mines." [1] The Mineral Point directory pointed out in 1859: "[W]hat is needed for their development, is capital employed as it is in England and Germany—where the mines extend . . . from 1,000 to more than 2,000 ft. deep."

The pressure of capital shortage in the lead region showed in the fact that a tremendous drop in sales accompanied the 1836 announcement that the federal government would receive only specie for federal lands. Some observers attributed the defection of lead miners to the California gold fields to the lack of capital to develop the lead area and provide steady employment.[2] In 1852 a legislative committee reported that mine drainage was lagging because such operations required an "aggregation and combination" of capital —more than the typical miner possessed. A year later another committee reported the same difficulty. The first annual report of the state geologist (1854) reported that lead mines were in a transitional period and needed capital to progress. From 1853 on, most of the annual governors' messages to the legislatures emphasized the great need. Opponents of bills designed to tighten the usury laws usually defeated such measures by arguing that lower legal rates of interest would dry up supplies of money.[3]

So went matters through the years. Capital was short; the mining industry needed investment funds badly; yet the industry's basic uncertainty, high risk, and its history of occasional unscrupulous promotions aggravated the problem. These same factors intensified demands that the law provide relief.

The first answer of law to these pleas for help was to provide a framework for a banking system for the territory and state. Banks served the mineral industry by collecting money from diverse sources —depositors and bank investors—and making this capital available to the industry by loans. For many years paper money floated by small state-chartered banking institutions made up the greatest part of western currency in circulation.

The history of a single bank, the Bank of Mineral Point, is important because this institution directly served the lead region. For a decade or two after it closed, its history affected the thinking of the state toward banks in particular and corporations in general. Its life story was repeated, with slight variations, in many other places.

Mineral Point was the center of the lead region. The federal land office was located there; the first lead deposit discovered in the territory was close by, as was the territorial capitol at Belmont. It was appropriate that the financial center be Mineral Point too.

On July 1, 1836 the United States Congress decreed: "[N]o act of the Territorial Legislature of any of the Territories of the United States, incorporating any bank or any institution with banking powers or privileges, hereafter to be passed, shall have any force or effect whatever, until approved and confirmed by Congress." [4] Act No. 10 of the First Wisconsin Territorial Legislature (1836) granted a twenty-one-year charter to the Mineral Point Bank with capitalization of $200,000. On March 3, 1837, Congress approved the charter, attaching conditions that (1) no bank notes might be circulated until one-half of the authorized capital had been paid in, (2) total authorized capital might not be increased without Congressional approval, and (3) the bank might not at "any time, owe, either by bond, bill, note, or other contract, over and above its actual de- posits, an amount to exceed twice the amount of its capital stock actually paid in." [5]

The bank began business when a great need for capital existed in the lead region. It issued a great number of bank notes to borrowers. For some time these bank notes passed at par, served as a medium of exchange, and stimulated the area's economy because of their inflationary effect. However, it was not long before creditors were unwilling to accept Mineral Point Bank notes at par. Matters were not aided by the bank's practice of issuing post notes, payable at a designated future time rather than on demand. "Red dog currency" (called so because the notes bore red print postponing the date of payment two or three months from the time of issuance) and "blue bellies" (on which blue printing announced that payment was postponed for six months) did not pass at par. Merchants of Galena, Illinois, paid miners for lead by using the bank's currency at par, but they "shaved," or discounted, the notes as much as 25 per cent when the miners returned them in payment for supplies. Soon miners refused to take the notes in payment for lead, arguing that they wanted metal in return for metal.

Public investigations in 1838 and 1839 cleared the bank of wrongdoing, but public confidence did not return. In the summer of 1841 the bank failed. One of its main promoters, cashier Samuel Knapp, fled to Galena. In 1839 Knapp leased the tower at Helena overlooking the Wisconsin River where lead shot of various sizes was made. From that time until his flight he successfully combined manufacturing and banking, buying lead and giving in exchange bank notes of the Mineral Point Bank. Most accounts of his flight report that he was captured after he gave a Galena newspaper editor two volumes of Dickens' novels which were later found to have bank assets pasted in their fly leaves. Another story was that the bank appointed W. H. Banks as its agent to go to St. Louis to collect bank securities, that he was never heard from again, and that this loss also fell upon depositors.

Investors and depositors in the bank and holders of the bank's notes lost almost all of their claims, totaling over $200,000. In 1841 the territorial legislature repealed the charter. Later official investigation led to the conclusion that the institution had not fully complied with the conditions laid down by Congress and that perhaps the bank began operation with no more tangible assets than its charter.

The failure of the Mineral Point Bank not only deprived the lead region of a sound credit system, but also nourished public hostility toward banks in particular and corporations in general, which was to continue for many years. A contemporary newspaper spoke in terms representative of public feeling:

[W]e opine that they . . . [the people] are not prepared to receive another scourging from the Bank of Mineral Point . . . or to approve of grand incorporations in the mining business with perpetual charters. We should be greatly disappointed if the legislature should charter any more companies and more surprised if the Governor should not veto them, and the people sustain him in so doing.[6]

After the bank's failure, the legislature followed a strict policy toward corporate charters. From 1839 to 1848 it chartered no mining corporations. In 1841 a committee of the territorial House recommended denying a charter to a corporation because the proposed language was "vague" and the company might "speculate in minerals."

Other reflections of legislative fear of the corporate device were provisions common in early charters, limiting corporate life, limiting total capitalization, and restricting the acreage the corporation might own. Pointing in the same direction were charter provisions which reserved power in the legislature to revoke charters for specified reasons. Some of these reservations were quite sweeping; one, for example, provided that the legislature might "alter, amend or repeal" the charter "whenever, in the opinion of . . . [the] Legislature, the interests of the people may require it." [7] The Wisconsin constitution (1848) further evidenced the mistrust of corporations, when it stipulated: "All general laws or special acts enacted under the provisions of this section . . . [authorizing the legislature to grant charters of incorporation] may be altered or repealed by the legislature at any time after their passage." [8]

Banking corporations were needed. A single failure here and there could not produce enough public sentiment against them to result in a lasting legal ban on their creation. Wisconsin's legislature continued to charter banks. The Civil War decade brought the next banking upheaval. By 1860 the state's banking laws required that bank owners deposit $25,000 of state or federal bonds with the state banking comptroller as a prerequisite to doing business. Although the state law also required $25,000 worth of working capital, bankers construed the deposit with the state comptroller as satisfying this requirement. Promoters organized many state banks in Wisconsin at out-of-the-way locations to provide some practical guarantee that their notes would not be presented for payment. Many bank owners used bonds of southern states to deposit with the comptroller. With the outbreak of war and defaults in these bonds, Wisconsin state bank notes were soon refused acceptance in the channels of trade. Many banks failed. In the lead region during the summer of 1861 miners, farmers, and mechanics would take nothing but specie in return for their products.

Gradually, with changes in the banking code made during the

Civil War and with the help of leading bankers of the eastern lake-front area of the state, some semblance of order was achieved and banks again became useful instruments to lend capital to miners and smelters. Although the Civil War experience of banking was severe, its impact upon the Wisconsin mining industry was not as calamitous as had been the failure of the Mineral Point Bank earlier. This was true because by 1860 the mineral industry was not dependent upon a single bank as it had been in 1840. From 1860 to the mid-twentieth century the state and federal history of banks and banking affected the mineral industry of Wisconsin, of course, but only in the same way it affected every other phase of the state's economy.

The law's second and greatest assistance in the mining industry's problem of capital scarcity was to make available the corporate form as an instrument for doing business. Law had created many corporations long before Wisconsin was settled, and Wisconsin law did not create anything novel for the mining industry. Some unusual suggestions about the powers and duties of corporations appeared about the mid-nineteenth century. For example, in 1848 a committee of the state senate urged that to protect citizens of the state as a whole and persons who might have direct relations with corporations, any Wisconsin general incorporation law should (1) limit the amount of land which the corporation might own, (2) provide for individual shareholder liability for corporate debts, (3) guarantee laborers working for the corporation the product of their labor, (4) guarantee members of the corporation—probably meaning the stockholders—a place to live on the domain of the company, and (5) guarantee the education of the children of the members of the corporation—probably meaning, at the expense of the corporation.[9] Had these ideas been implemented, Wisconsin corporations would have become much more than just forms for doing business. However, under the laws as they stood from 1850 on, the corporate device remained strictly a business instrument.

Considering the risks involved in the search for minerals, one might suppose that mining businessmen were influenced in using the corporate device by a desire to insulate their non-corporate assets from personal liability following failures. Prior to 1872, when under a new constitutional limitation the legislature ceased granting individual charters by special acts, very few special charters stated limitations upon the personal liability of stockholders. In fact, an 1853 charter expressly provided: "[T]he stockholders shall be individually liable for debts contracted by said company." [10] Other sweeping charters contained waivers of limited liability. Thus one style of charter provided: "The Stockholders . . . shall be jointly and individually liable, for all debts that may be due and owing to any of their clerks, labor[er]s, or servants for services performed for such corporation." [11] The inclusion of these express waivers of limited liability indicate that in a large number of instances the corporate device was chosen for reasons other than the desire to limit personal liability, or at least despite imposition of some liability.

The chief reason dictating use of the corporation was that it enabled mining promoters to collect capital from diverse and numerous sources and to bring the investment under the management of a relatively small number of people, either the officers or the board of directors. The table on page 85, which includes all special mining charters granted between 1836, when Wisconsin Territory was formed, and 1872, when an effective general incorporation act was passed, illustrates the widespread use of the corporation in the mining industry.

Prior to 1853 mining in the lead region was simple and cheap. But by that year many mines in the area had reached water level, the large labor migration to California had increased labor costs, and the mines were at a transition period in which they needed capital for future development. There was a real connection between these conditions and the number of special charters.

Commonly, special charters were of the same pattern; they often read word for word alike where circumstances did not require variation in terms. Draftsmen obviously followed form books or copied from the statute books. Promoters wanted speed; it was easy to persuade the legislature to pass the commonplace and risky to ask for something different. Thus, there were many reasons why the "special" acts had less that was special in their content, compared one with another, than might be expected.

Inherently the corporate device lent itself to pooling the capital

SPECIAL MINING CHARTERS GRANTED, 1836–1871

Year	Iron, Lead & Copper	Oil	Coal, Clay & Stone	Peat	Gold & Silver	Amendments to Charters	Total
1836	2						2
1838	5					1	6
1848	1					1	2
1852	1						1
1853	16					1	17
1854	15					1	16
1855	5					2	7
1856	9						9
1857	1						1
1858	1					4	5
1859	2					3	5
1860						1	1
1861	1						1
1862	1						1
1863	4						4
1864	1					4	5
1865	19	23				3	45
1866	26	41	2	10	6	3	88
1867	22	3		8	2	6	41
1868	8					4	12
1869	4		2	1		1	8
1870	9		2		3	1	15
1871	12		1			4	17
Total	165	67	7	19	11	40	309

contributions of many and channeling their use to a single aim. In addition to this fact, special charters granted by the Wisconsin legislature prior to 1872 contained other provisions which made them more efficient devices for pooling capital. Drafted by the mineral promoters themselves and seldom altered by the legislature, these charters vividly portrayed the capital scarcity, and the attack upon it.

All special-charter mining companies possessed a capital structure consisting of common stock only. This characteristic pertained, not because the laws of Wisconsin required it, but because it satisfied the needs of mineral promoters and fitted well the prevailing frontier philosophy. Preferred stock with its prior guaranteed return and preference in case of business failure, shared fewer of the risks of ownership than common stock, and thus was in opposition to the frontier attitude that all should share the same risks whether the risks stemmed from Indians or from business failures. Frontier society was not stratified, class lines were not distinct, and the lack of an investor class interested only in preferred stock was an application of the prevailing ideas of democracy and equality. Furthermore, since there existed no class of investors interested in buying only preferred stock, mineral promoters' needs were satisfied with a capital structure featuring only common stock.

Most charters permitted stockholders to buy stock on time payments. The subscriber made a down payment and the balance was payable on the call of the corporation. An 1854 provision is typical: "[The directors may determine] the time, manner, and proportion which the stockholders shall pay for the shares of stock subscribed by them, and forfeit to the use of the company the share or shares of any person failing to pay any installment at a reasonable period, not less than thirty days after the time by them appointed for the payment thereof." [12]

Such a provision permitted the corporation to lay first claim to any future capital accumulated by existing stockholders. Some planning for the future by corporations was possible because of this regular procedure for mobilizing additional funds; the penalty of forfeiture gave some assurance that calls would be met, especially after stockholders had paid in enough to build a real equity. This advantage was offset by the disadvantage that calls were most necessary in times of corporate financial distress, which more often than not coincided with times when stockholders themselves were financially embarrassed. This fact may have been a contributing cause of the recurring panics of the nineteenth century.

Many charters expressly permitted the issuance of corporate stock in exchange for real and personal property. This was an innocuous and, indeed, useful provision as long as the value of the stock issued bore a fair relation to the property given in payment. By this technique promoters eliminated the need to raise capital to buy land and personal property.

However, the absence in the charter of any requirement that the value of the property received by the corporation bear some fair relation to the value of the stock given in exchange permitted unfair practices. A stockholder exchanging property for stock could be overcompensated for his property, and the voting rights and share of ownership of existing stockholders substantially diluted.

A few corporate charters exempted companies from the regular usury laws. In the nineteenth century, competition for capital was keen. Promoters who could offer the greatest return in interest were preferred by lenders. The high risks that attended the mineral industry worsened its competitive position in the race for capital, and exemptions from the usury laws were a great boon.

In the 1880's when northern Wisconsin mining areas were being developed, proponents of increased legal interest rates argued that higher rates in other states left Wisconsin's mining industry without adequate money. In 1880 a bill proposed to alter the legal rate of interest. A committee report pointed out that higher rates permitted in adjoining states were siphoning off capital needed by Wisconsin enterprises. Mining suffered especially, according to the report, because it carried the added disadvantage of high risk. The report concluded that a provision lowering the legal interest rate would check the development of the state's natural resources. Usury laws, according to the report, were "relics of the dark ages and worse than useless." This strong indictment of the usury laws did not satisfy a minority which urged that the usury laws all be repealed, arguing, "We have brains, energy and enterprise. What we need is money." [13]

However, with opinion divided, nothing drastic was done to the usury laws beyond the few special-charter provisions which exempted their beneficiaries from the regular usury regulations. Occasionally, one of these exemptions provoked a governor to veto the offending charter. To the extent that these exemptions became law, inequality was written piecemeal into the law, with individual companies receiving favors which most of the mining industry failed to obtain. Sufficient pressure from the public and industry to modify the usury laws to allow higher interest rates may have failed to materialize because, as Abraham Lincoln pointed out, a usury law did not "materially injure any class . . . for in extreme cases where excessive interest might be justified, means could be found to evade the law." [14]

"Borrowed" capital, as distinguished from "ownership" capital, supplied some of the miners' needs. Special charters were liberal in conferring the power to borrow. Broad grants, such as the following provision in the charter of the St. Croix River Mining Company granted in 1866, typically included the power to issue bonds secured by a "mortgage or deed of trust conveying all of . . . [the corporation's] property, real, personal and mixed and all of its corporate rights, franchises and privileges." [15]

Some charter provisions were designed to foster the public's enthusiasm for investing by making it easier for small investors to risk their savings. Par values were kept low: five-dollar and ten-dollar shares were the rule. The fact that elaborate, engraved stock certificates were received in exchange for small monetary outlays generated public excitement. Corporate treasuries grew because of many small stock purchases. Charters often authorized large total capitalization—to totals of $1,000,000, $2,000,000, or $3,000,000—and thus encouraged investors to a sanguine outlook for an expanding future.

The contribution that the corporate form made in alleviating the shortage of capital cannot obscure the fact that its use was financially and socially costly. The cost was great, especially during the years when each incorporation required passage of a special legislative bill. There was expended on this matter an enormous amount of valuable legislative time which should have been spent on other items of public importance. Some of the most familiar characteristics of American legislatures—such as the end-of-session jam of bills which typically produced delay or neglect of pressing public matters, and poor craftsmanship in the drafting of general laws—resulted directly from the burdensome detail that attended the issuing of special charters.

Between 1848 and 1871 the Wisconsin legislature granted 1,130 special charters covering all types of business activities. These were not evenly distributed through the years. For example, in 1866 an extremely large demand swelled to over 1,444 pages the statute book which contained special laws. This volume included 88 mining charters.

Conceivably the legislature might have used its control of the terms of incorporation to establish extensive control over large areas of the economy, including direction of the sparse supply of capital, but legislators made little or no use of this potential power. Most charters were stereotyped legal documents which covered only the business essentials and which conformed to the needs of private draftsmen. Even when charters went beyond the provisions absolutely necessary for private corporate management, they dealt only piecemeal with matters of great public importance. For example, some mining charters contained general criminal and civil law provisions. The 1852 charter of the Mineral Point Railway required that trespassers upon company property pay treble damages; the 1853 charter of the Dodgeville Mining and Manufacturing Company made such trespasses a misdemeanor; the 1863 charter of the Penokee Mining and Railroad Company provided that if a trespasser on company property caused a death, the homicide was first-degree murder. Sometimes a special charter included tax levies. Such provisions illustrate the scope of legislative control which would have been possible within the framework of incorporation. At the same time, the examples show how important decisions on matters of wide public concern were rendered piecemeal as individual charters came before the legislatures.

Special charters customarily gave little protection to creditors of the company. Although the charters usually stipulated that some minimum part of the capital stock be paid in before business might commence, the designated sums were very low. Ordinary provisions conditioned the beginning of business on the subscription of $4,000 out of $50,000 authorized capital stock, or upon the subscription of $50,000 of capital stock and the actual payment into the corporation of 5 per cent of that amount in cash. In the light of the corporate theory that property paid in for capital stock is a trust fund to which creditors of the corporation may look for payment of their claims, the fund was often inadequate and sometimes almost completely illusory. Large authorized capitalizations were accompanied in actual practice by very little cash received in exchange for stock totalling a large par value. This fact made dealing with a corporation a hazardous venture for creditors.

A few special charters specifically protected creditors (often only a limited class of creditors, such as laborers) by making the stockholders individually liable to them for corporate debts. Where stock was exchanged for assets other than money, creditors sometimes suffered because property contributed in exchange for stock did not equal either the par or market value of the stock given in exchange. An 1891 case dealt with the rights of unsatisfied judgment creditors of a mining company which had issued shares worth ten times the property received for the shares. The creditors sued the stockholders who were parties to the transaction. The Wisconsin Supreme Court stated:

> In an action against the stockholders of a corporation to compel them to contribute to the payment of the debts of the insolvent corporation it is only necessary, in order to make out a *prima facie* case, to establish the fact that the stockholder has not in good faith paid the par value for his stock to the corporation. . . .
>
> "The idea that the capital of a corporation is a football, to be thrown into the market for speculation, that its value may be elevated or depressed to advance the interests of its managers, is a modern and wicked invention." [16]

Existing shareholders possessed little protection against intentional excesses and flagrant mistakes of managers. Few, if any, special mining charters specifically granted stockholders a right to inspect corporate books. Rare was the charter that protected existing shareholders' proportionate voting power by granting them a prior right to subscribe to new stock issues. No court case involving a mining company determined whether the judiciary would create protection for stockholders in these two areas.

As might be imagined, in view of the great need for capital and the risky nature of mining, the investing public suffered severe losses in several mining booms. Many lost money in the Civil War oil boom. In a two-year period, during 1865 and 1866, the legislature charted sixty-four oil companies. Many were capitalized in excess of $1,000,000. Among the 6,648 residents of Madison were those who poured $200,000 into oil stocks; the total for the entire state must have run into millions. No terms of any oil charter provided a basis for coping with the overreaching and fraudulent practices that accompanied oil promotion. The law was neutral in the critical stages of promotion, and took the side neither of the promoter nor of the investor until after promotion ran to a ruinous end. Then the law provided a suit for damages for fraud or breach of contract, if such could be proved. Not one suit of this nature came to the Wisconsin Supreme Court from the oil episode.

The second great wave of stock selling and financial loss occurred twenty years later. As noted in Chapter 1, credit for the discovery of iron ore on the Penokee-Gogebic range on the Upper Michigan border belongs to Captain N. D. Moore, although Increase Lapham earlier had reported that the area's potential was great. Moore, in 1872, found hematite under the roots of a tree felled by a tornado near the present city of Bessemer, Michigan. After the discovery, Moore entered lands in both Michigan and Wisconsin, and participated in the formation of several companies to exploit the deposits. On the Wisconsin side of the boundary line, great interest built up and the boom reached its zenith in 1886.

A strip of land, which in 1884 was only a blazed right-of-way for a railroad, became the main street of Ironwood, Wisconsin, in 1886. Hurley, Wisconsin, came into being complete with a newspaper, the *Iron Tribune,* and brick stores. Prospective purchasers and investors signed up for special excursions to the area; fifteen thousand people came to settle the region. Speculators and promoters used almost every trick of the trade to sell shares and property. A large map with red and blue lines purporting to show the extent of the iron ore deposit was often exhibited to would-be investors and purchasers. Most of them believed that the map was prepared by the United States Geological Survey. Naturally, almost every property offered to investors appeared well within the boundaries of the red and blue lines. When explorations failed to find ore, the explanation was that the lines were not correctly drawn, that there was a scientific margin of error, or that the ore deposit pitched downward sharply and the shaft did not reach deep enough. All three explanations laid the groundwork for a plea for more financial support.

For a time the Gogebic operation in Wisconsin was the main topic of conversation in Madison, Milwaukee, and smaller towns of the state. Optimism was the keynote—operations at a named location were "panning out big," a new stock issue was "nabbed up quick," and stock advances of 100 per cent in two days were carefully noted and acted upon. Told in the words of a contemporary:

The story of the rise and collapse of the Gogebic boom is a dramatic episode in the financial history of the State. A people noted for business conservatism yielded to insane excitement when an opportunity seemed to offer untold wealth without paying its equivalent. The "boom" had its center in Milwaukee, and while the speculative craze over the properties reached beyond the State in many directions, the majority of the victims were in Wisconsin. Millionaires were made in a day and bankruptcy followed in the night. It was stated at the time that three-fourths of the professional men in Milwaukee and fully seven-eighths of the business-men were involved. Homes were mortgaged or sold, savings from hard-earned salaries were withdrawn from banks, money was borrowed—all to be invested in Gogebic stock.

. . . Speculators did some heavy work. More than one forty beyond what was understood to be the line of the ore vein was marked by pits and shafts. Holes were dug and immediately upon striking ore the owner would capitalize at from $100,000 to $1,000,000. Elegantly engraved certificates of stock were at once placed upon the market. The par value of a share would be $25, and it would be sold for from $1 to $3 a share in order, as the promotors claimed, to secure money to proceed with the work. All the devices used from time immemorial whereby something might be got for nothing were brought into play . . . stock exchanges . . . were established in Milwaukee and Chicago.[17]

The crash came in the fall of 1887. Stock prices gradually fell and soon plummeted. Corporate treasuries were depleted and exploration halted. Many companies held their ore ranges under leases which required a continuous exploration program, and under which royalty payments were due even before ore was found. Empty corporate treasuries led to a cessation of exploration and royalty payments. Forfeitures of leases followed. When the public learned this fact, stock values dropped out of sight. In some instances honest men and locations which later proved rich were caught in the downswing. As the writer quoted above appraised the situation:

> The majority of those who were exploiting the range were sincere enough. Several of them risked and lost every dollar of their own, a fact which vouched for their faith if not for their judgment. And it is not to be inferred that all trading in stock was inherently dishonest. There were promoters who tried to keep within the range of legitimate transactions and did; there were others who tried to do so and did not seem to know when the tide of speculation carried them from their moorings.[18]

Again, law was neutral between promoter and investor in the critical stage of their active relation. Law did nothing to protect the investor before loss and nothing to require the promoter to adhere to minimum standards of morality and honesty during the promotion.

Unlike the oil boom a few years earlier, the Gogebic promotion spawned law suits. One of these cases, *Warner* v. *Bates* (1889), illustrates clearly the typical promotion tactics used, as well as the inadequacy of law to protect the investor. A Mr. and Mrs. Benjamin, a Mr. and Mrs. Bates, and a Mr. N. D. Moore (probably the same person who discovered ore on the Gogebic range) formed a company (Moore, Benjamin & Company) to engage in buying and selling mining stocks in Milwaukee. Mrs. Warner alleged that she lived in Milwaukee and that she was a good social friend of Mr. and Mrs. Benjamin. Mrs. Warner complained that she had placed the utmost confidence in the advice of the Benjamins and that they had "unlawfully, wickedly, and maliciously conspir[ed] . . . to procure . . . [Mrs. Warner] to sell . . . her real estate . . . and . . . purchase . . . certain . . . mining stocks, and thereby to cheat and defraud . . . [Mrs. Warner]."

This allegation preceded a long list of false and fraudulent representations which, Mrs. Warner stated, induced her to buy the stock: statements affirming that the issuing corporation had at least one-half of its capital stock subscribed, that it owned valuable mineral lands that were highly productive, that the stocks were safe, and that Mrs. Warner could not possibly lose anything, but instead stood to reap a great increase in stock value.

Twice the case came before the state supreme court. The first time the court refused to pass upon the truth of Mrs. Warner's allegations, holding only that the arrest of Mr. Bates, a nonresident, to prevent him from leaving the state was authorized by state law.[19]

At the second trial Mrs. Warner proved her allegations, and the jury awarded her a judgment for over $15,000. The Wisconsin Supreme Court reversed this judgment upon two grounds. First, the appellate court concluded that the trial court had erred in excluding defense evidence that Mrs. Warner bought after she had counselled with others who had advised her of the risk, and, indeed, had advised her not to purchase the stock. The court considered this relevant because:

If the plaintiff . . . [Mrs. Warner] had knowledge of the actual facts, or had knowledge of such facts as would have led to the discovery of the truth by the use of reasonable diligence, and failed to use such diligence, she cannot now say that she was defrauded in the purchase.[20]

Secondly, the supreme court concluded that the jury had erred in assessing as plaintiff's damages the amount she had paid for the stock, even if it were true that, as Mrs. Warner alleged, the stocks were of "no value whatsoever" at the time of the trial.

> The well-established rule [of damages] . . . upon a sale of . . . property which is voidable on account of fraudulent representations is the difference between the *real value* of the article sold at the time of the sale and what the value would have been had the representations been true. . . . [T]he market value of the stock at or about the time of the sale is undoubtedly evidence bearing on the question of its *real value,* although not necessarily conclusive. [Italics added.] [21]

This holding, which measured Mrs. Warner's damages by asking whether she paid about what other investors were paying for the same stock at the time she purchased, reduced almost to impotence the civil remedy for fraud and deceit.

The Gogebic boom wasted capital. Royalty payments on forfeited leases which never produced, advertising expenses, tours to northern areas, badly located shafts and tunnels were only a small part of the waste. More important, the many fraudulent ventures gave mining stocks a bad reputation which lasted for years.

Other Gogebic cases in the supreme court presented legal issues growing out of corporate promotions. In one case a stockholder claimed that promoters received $90,000 from the corporation for a mining option which cost the vendors $20,000. In another suit, corporate creditors sought to hold stockholders liable for corporate debts upon the ground that the par value of shares received in exchange for property transferred to the corporation was many times the value of the property.

The two major evils accompanying the use of corporations to provide capital were the waste involved in granting charters by special acts and the lack of any effective sanctions to deal with the fraud that was often associated with mining booms. The special charter problem was eliminated in the nineteenth century, and regulation of the integrity of investment promotions waited upon twentieth-century developments.

Article XI, Section 1, of the original 1848 Wisconsin constitution provided that "corporations . . . shall not be created by special act, except for municipal purposes, and in cases where, in the judgment of the legislature, the objects of the corporation cannot be attained under general laws." For twenty-four years the limiting language of this provision proved of no effect. Legislatures ignored it by routine recitations that corporate objects could not be attained under general laws. This conclusion did not rest on the fact that general laws were unavailable, but, if it rested on any logical base at all, on the conclusion that general laws contained restrictions and limitations which incorporators did not desire.

The Wisconsin Revised Statutes, 1849, included a general incorporation law. However, this act limited corporate life to thirty years, prohibited real estate holding in excess of forty acres for each stockholder and forbade mortgaging or giving a lien upon corporate assets. It made stockholders individually liable for the corporate debts for labor, and for other debts of the corporation reduced to judgment, when an execution was returned unsatisfied. The statute said that only money might be accepted in payment for stock. In view of these restrictions, it was small wonder that promoters did not desire to incorporate under this general law.

A joint stock company act passed in 1853 limited capital to $300,000 and made stockholders individually liable for claims of laborers for work done within six months prior to the demand. Though promoters objected to these limitations, the 1853 act did eliminate the other restrictions contained in the 1849 law, and this difference induced many mining companies to form under the joint stock company act. By 1865 and 1866, however, the trend swung back to special acts and in those two years some mining companies which had previously organized under the joint stock company act sought and obtained special charters.

In 1866 the state enacted a general incorporation law for corporations mining, smelting, and manufacturing iron, copper, lead, zinc, silver, or other ores or minerals. Restrictions included a limit of thirty years on corporate life, a minimum capital of $10,000 and a maximum capital of $500,000, a limit of 5,000 acres permitted total real estate holdings, the liability of individual stockholders to laborers possessing unsatisfied judgments against the corporation, and a special tax in lieu of all other state taxes. The special tax was a tonnage tax on all ore "obtained"; the rates were fixed at $1.00 per ton on copper, 10 cents on iron, and 25 cents on lead. Any inducement to use the general law because of this tax advantage soon disappeared when drafters of special charters began writing the same tax into their documents.

Before 1870 a few governors and some legislatures showed hostility to the special charter device. In 1851 Governor Dewey vetoed a bill incorporating a mining company, stating, "The general laws provide for the organization of companies to conduct this business which answers all the purposes of this bill." [22] In 1858 Governor Randall vetoed a charter upon the same ground. In 1863 Governor Salomon stated three grounds for vetoing an act incorporating a mining company: (1) the objects could be obtained under the general laws; (2) the company was specifically exempted from the usury law; and (3) there was no provision in the special charter as there was under the general laws that the stockholders were liable in certain cases for debts of the company. The governor observed that if the general laws were too stringent, they should be amended. A few days later he vetoed another mining bill and complained that the constitutional prohibition against special incorporations stood "as a mockery."

During the next administration, 1864, no one applied a check rein. But the flood of charters was such as to stir some legislative determination to stop the practice. In 1867 the assembly committee on incorporations recommended indefinite postponement of the first mining charter request laid before it. By this action, the committee sought to establish an example for the balance of the session. The committee reported that the practice of issuing special charters had cost the state "thousands upon thousands" of dollars and that existing general laws were ample to cover all legitimate business desires.

Governor Fairchild's annual message in 1870 stated that too much "needless" and "pernicious" special legislation passed each year. A month later Fairchild amplified his views in a special message to the legislature in which he proposed a constitutional ban on special business charters. He estimated that an effective ban would reduce by two-thirds the number of bills passed and would free legislative time for "matters of general concern." This legislature and its successor responded by adopting and submitting to the people a constitutional amendment which was approved on popular referendum in 1871. The constitutional amendment stipulates: "The legislature is prohibited from enacting any special or private laws in the following cases: . . . 7th. For granting corporate powers or privileges, except to cities." [23]

Concurrently with this ban the legislature passed a new general incorporation law. The new bill lacked many of the restrictions which had in the past made promoters dissatisfied with charters under the general laws. Thus, after 1871 Wisconsin legislatures were no longer burdened with requests for special mining charters.

Through the nineteenth century legal relief for fraud committed in selling mining stocks consisted only of private suits for damages or a public prosecution under the general statutes condemning the obtaining of money or property by false pretenses. These remedies were available only after a tainted transaction was completed and the harm inflicted. In view of the history of the oil boom and the Gogebic experience, it is not surprising that initial attempts to broaden legal measures to prevent fraud in business finance were limited to dealings in mining stocks. The 1905, 1909, and 1911 legislative sessions saw the introduction of bills specifically aimed at vendors of mining stocks. In 1913 the state embarked upon the first of a long course of legislation designed to insure honest and fair dealing in the sale of all corporate stocks, whether for mining or for other ventures.

After 1913 legislative efforts were directed toward preventing fraud by requiring that accurate, factual data be supplied the investing public. Such emphasis on preventive measures, rather than merely on reparative, was a marked change in policy. Because the new policy was broad in reach and sought affirmatively to create a healthier investment situation, a new approach to enforcement was required.

The legislature applied a new sanction by (1) employing the flexible device of requiring a license for the sale of stock in Wisconsin and (2) assigning to an administrative agency—the Railroad Commission—administration of the licensing system.

The new securities law required any firm or individual selling, offering for sale, or negotiating for sale any security to procure a license from the commission. The act further provided: "No such license shall be issued to any dealer . . . whose business is so conducted as to deceive or mislead investors or the public, nor unless its business is conducted in all respects in good faith and in compliance with law, and whenever the contrary shall appear to said commission the license theretofore issued shall be revoked." [24]

The law required any company seeking to sell its own securities to file stipulated information with the commission and to have the approval of the commission for all printed matter which the company desired to circulate. One provision in particular was designed to strike down practices common in mining promotions:

No person for the purpose of organizing or promoting any company . . . shall sell . . . any securities . . . unless the contract of subscription . . . shall be in writing and contain a provision in the following language:
(b) No sum shall be used for commission, promotion and organization expense . . . in this company in excess of —— per cent of the amount actually paid up on separate subscriptions for such securities and the remainder . . . shall be held or invested as authorized by . . . law . . . and held by organizers . . . , and the directors and officers of such company after organization as bailees for the subscriber, to be used only in the conduct of the business for which such company is organized.[25]

This provision sought to insure that stockholders would be fully informed what part of their payment would be used for promoter's expenses and what part would eventually be left for the business of the company. Although technical changes were made in the law after 1913, its basic premise remained undisturbed. None of the legislative changes in later years reflected any consideration directly related to peculiarities of the mining business.

Although law's major contribution to the problem of capital

scarcity was to make available the corporate instrument, law also supplied the formal framework for other modes of doing business. As early as 1837 the territorial legislature adopted a partnership act for mining and smelting operations. This legislation favored mining ventures by allowing the creation of limited partnerships under which some partners might limit the amount of their liability against the contingency of failure. The territorial act was the only partnership legislation in Wisconsin which was specifically addressed to the mining industry. After statehood, mining partnerships fell under general partnership laws not tailored to any special mining issue. Public records, which tell a good deal about mining corporations, tell little about how much the mining industry used either the territorial partnership law or the general state partnership legislation.

5

The Human Element

LAND, CAPITAL, AND labor had to be brought into effective combination to produce, refine, and market Wisconsin's minerals. The labor factor produced fewer problems for the legal order than either of the other two elements. But if problems affecting labor were not numerous, they touched vital human interests.

This chapter will not cover exhaustively the entire legal history of the problems of mining labor.[1] Instead, several areas of particular importance to the mineral industry will be discussed. In most areas of the law's relation to labor, the history of problems not discussed here, such as minimum wages, maximum hours, unemployment compensation, government-financed employment offices, disputes between labor and management, and apprentice training, paralleled the history of the same problems in other industries.

The major legal problems concerning labor to be discussed fall into two main areas: (1) allocating losses accompanying industrial accidents and diseases; (2) employing governmental power to protect laborers from industrial injuries and the ravages of occupational diseases.

Logically these two areas were not unrelated. The more strictly the law assessed accident costs against employers, for example, the more likely it was that employers would concern themselves to create safer working conditions and to make more careful selection of competent co-workers. However, through the nineteenth century, legal doctrine did not acknowledge this logical connection. Instead, prior to 1911 the social costs of accidents and diseases attributed to mining were distributed through litigation according to concepts of fault and counterfault. Neither the courts nor the legislature attempted to assess the effect that law's cost allocations might have in promoting safer working conditions.

First, let us examine the history of law's distribution of the costs arising from mining accidents. Prior to 1911, of the three branches of state government, the judiciary alone performed the task of distributing accident costs. The judges performed this function by deciding law suits between individuals, usually an employee and an employer. That the allocation issue was thus presented piecemeal for public decision making through individual law suits intensified law's inability to assess the overall problem.

The first mining accident case appeared in the Wisconsin Supreme Court in 1872. Mining activity in Wisconsin reached back to the 1820's and 1830's, and by 1872 the rise and fall of the lead mines was history. However, prior to 1872 mining was largely surface mining and was done under physical conditions not conducive to many accidents. Deep mining, which produced more opportunities for serious accidents, occurred later. Furthermore, much early mining was done by individual miners who worked their own diggings. In this state of operations, with no differentiation of miners and mine owners, there was no occasion for law suits by individual injured employees against employers. Finally, frontier conditions and philosophy were against such law suits. Frequently, an employee in the early mines was a neighbor who worked for a short time for a mine owner who lived close by. Often the employee's compensation took the form of return labor. Under these conditions an employee viewed any injuries suffered as his own responsibility, and many possible law suits were never filed.

A brief survey of the mine accident cases in the Wisconsin Supreme Court from 1872 to 1911 discloses the nature of the risks involved as well as the legal rules which the judges developed to settle disputes and allocate the costs of injuries. The cases discussed below are those appealed to the state supreme court, because that is the only state court whose opinions were published. These cases represent a small portion of the total mining accidents and may not present an accurate cross section of events in the period covered. But at this distance in time, they represent the most available and reliable evidence of the nature of the problem.

Prior to 1911 the foundation of liability for unintended personal injury was fault. If an injured miner were to have the law's help to shift his loss, he must demonstrate that his injuries resulted from the defendant's failure to conduct himself in a reasonable manner. Generally the alleged fault consisted of the employer's failure to provide the injured person with safe tools or a safe place to work, or in neglecting to notify the worker of unsafe conditions.

Even if the employer's fault was established within legal concepts, the injured employee faced three possible defenses, any of which would relieve the employer of liability: contributory negligence, assumption of risk, and the fellow-servant rule. Both the initial burden of proof on the plaintiff and the scope of these defenses were potent in protecting employers from liability.

In the first case (1872) a mine shaft caved in and crippled a copper miner for life. He secured judgment upon a jury verdict for $900 and successfully retained it when the defendant-employer appealed on the grounds that the injured miner had assumed the risk of cracks in the shaft. The court deemed crucial the miner's evidence that the employer knew the crack existed, and failed to warn the employee of this danger.[2]

A boy less than fifteen years old, employed to carry tools from a mine to a nearby blacksmith shop, suffered the loss of a leg when a large rock fall crushed it. In 1886 the supreme court determined that he might recover. His youth defeated the employer's defense that the boy had assumed the risk of falling rock.[3]

In 1891 the supreme court decided against a car loader whose right thigh, ankle, and left leg were broken by a rock fall as he was helping place scaffolding in a mine tunnel. Assumption of risk barred his recovery of damages.[4]

A lead-region miner was injured when he drilled into an unexploded charge set several days previously. A lower court judgment in his favor was reversed when the supreme court, in 1898, decided that the jury should have considered whether a fellow miner noticed the unexploded charge and failed to give warning.[5] This was the fellow-servant rule in operation.

In 1900 the court denied recovery to a miner who was hit when a tub used in hoisting ore fell down a vertical shaft. The court found that the fellow employee who ran the hoisting mechanism had not used care in its operation.[6] Once again the fellow-servant rule operated. A 1906 decision refused recovery for the death of a steam engine stoker who fell one hundred feet into an unguarded shaft.[7] The deceased had noticed the unsafe condition before the accident and requested the employer to remedy it. The court decided that after the employer had failed for a reasonable length of time to erect guards, the employee again assumed the risk. Stripped of all verbal refinements, the holding granted immunity to employers who delayed long enough after an employee complained of unsafe working conditions.

A miner climbing an inclined mine shaft was killed when he met a car racing down. His estate recovered $2,500. In 1907 the supreme court reversed this award, holding that deceased had contributed to his own death.[8] This was the defense of contributory negligence.

In four other cases decided after 1910, employees successfully protected lower court judgments in their favor. These cases included a smelting plant worker, scalded when a ladle filled with molten metal tipped; a miner who lost his leg when it was crushed by ore falling from a roof; a twenty-five-year-old miner incapacitated permanently by falling rock; and a worker whose arm was torn from his body when it was drawn between a belt and a pulley.[9]

We lack the data from which to strike a total of persons injured by mining accidents. Many cases were settled by trial court adjudication; many more by out-of-court settlements. Records of these are either nonexistent or widely scattered. The supreme court cases just discussed amply demonstrate that people were killed and severely injured in mining and that the applicable common-law doctrine made it hard to shift these losses to others.

The rules which the Wisconsin courts thus applied in law suits growing out of injuries suffered by miners on the job were all borrowed from doctrines developed out of the problems of other areas of human activity. These rules were not specially created to adjust to the situation of mining accident cases. They governed most cases in which physically injured persons sought to recover damages from others.

Though Anglo-American law had, of course, for centuries recognized fault as the basis for liability, the body of common-law doctrine which the Wisconsin courts applied in the mining accident cases before 1911 expressed value judgments in favor of those taking the initiative for productive action and in favor of invested capital, which reflected the capital scarcity and the emphasis on production of the nineteenth-century United States. Though judicial opinions did not commonly make plain that they were subordinating the interests of individual workers in their personal productive capacity and the interests of the affected individuals and of the society in the integrity of the families of breadwinners, this subordination was implicit in the decisions. This allocation of values did not, of course, eliminate the costs to workers, families, and community of the values thus subordinated to capital growth and investment. But, at least by the third quarter of the nineteenth century, the pattern of judicial precedent was too firmly set to be changed other than by legislation.

In 1911 the Wisconsin legislature acted.[10] Mining accidents did not, alone, produce the change. Through the years other industries contributed their share to the total record of broken bodies and grieving survivors as costs of the machine age. But mining accidents formed an important part of the past which prompted the new legislation.

The policy behind the 1911 statute was entirely unlike any of the judge-made rules which had governed for over half a century. Swept away were most of the old ideas of fault and counterfault. The new act was based upon the policy that industrial accidents were as much a cost of doing business as machinery breakdowns and casualty losses of physical assets.

The 1911 Workmen's Compensation Act in Wisconsin applied to private employment only if the employer elected to come under the statute. The voluntary nature of the 1911 law grew out of fears that a compulsory law would be held unconstitutional. The act was mandatory when the state, counties, towns, cities, villages, or school districts were employers. There seems to be no record that any of these governmental units engaged in widespread mining or in refining minerals, and the mandatory part of the first law had little impact on the legal history of mining. Private employers were free to consent to be governed by the law or not. In operation, however, their choice was considerably curtailed. Section 1 of the act deprived any employer electing to stand outside the law of two time-honored defenses. He might no longer defend himself either on the ground that the injured employee had assumed the risk of the hazard which injured him or on the ground that the injury was caused by the want of ordinary care of a fellow servant. Thus, the statute induced employers to come under it by denying non-consenting employers two ancient defensive strongholds of employers, the defenses of assumption of risk and the fellow-servant rule. A 1913 amendment put further compulsion upon employers by taking away the defense of contributory negligence.[11] The law prohibited contracts, rules, or regulations which sought to waive these statutory changes.

The language of the 1911 act also granted employees the right to choose whether or not to be governed by the act. However, an employee remaining outside its provisions was required to prove that the employer's fault caused the injury and required to prove the amount of damages. Between 1911 and 1913, he was also subject to the doctrine of contributory negligence. Thus, the statutory pattern induced employees to consent, because under the act, instead of needing to prove his employer's fault the claimant needed only to prove that he was "performing service growing out of and incidental to his employment" at the time he was injured. The act continued to absolve employers for injuries caused by the employee's *willful* misconduct—probably a rare occurrence and of little practical importance. If both employer and employee consented to the act, it was the exclusive remedy for the injuries.

The act also changed the method of measuring the monetary loss suffered by the injured employee. Under the pre-1911, judge-made law, juries awarded damages based upon the general theory of restoring the injured man to the position he occupied before the accident—as nearly as a lump sum of money would accomplish that objective. Much courtroom time was consumed in producing evidence and deciding issues about hospital and doctor bills, total and partial disability, permanent and temporary handicaps, the money value of pain and suffering, and life expectancy. All these facts must be explored as the prerequisite to jury determination of the amount of the plaintiff's recovery. Under this system jury verdicts varied greatly for substantially similar injuries.

The 1911 act substituted new uniform measures of recovery. If the employee was not fatally injured, the benefits payable were (1) the expenses of medical and surgical care, including crutches and other similar apparatus, for a period of ninety days, (2) 65 per cent of the employee's weekly loss in wages if the disability were partial, and (3) 65 per cent of the employee's average weekly earnings for the disability period if the disability were total (the 65 per cent figure advanced to 100 per cent after the first ninety days if the employee's condition required the service of a nurse). The act's requirement that payments be made weekly, commencing shortly after the injury, eliminated an injustice which was inherent in the pre-1911 rules of liability. Before 1911 an employee might wait a year or more before any money came into his possession. Even if the plaintiff won his suit, litigation took time, and meanwhile living expenses did not stop.

The three items of recovery were subject to two overall limitations. First, aggregate recovery by an employee for a single accident might not exceed four times his average annual earnings. Second, the aggregate disability might not extend beyond fifteen years from the date of the accident.

When the accident caused death, benefits payable included the benefits already listed, which were payable until death terminated the disability period, plus an additional sum depending on whether the deceased left dependents and whether they were wholly or partially dependent upon him for support. If no dependents were left, the death benefit amounted to reasonable burial expenses, not to exceed one hundred dollars.

The act created a new government body—the Industrial Commission—to administer the law.[12] The board was staffed by three paid officials. This new board assumed a variety of duties under the act. By far the most important of these were hearing injury disputes, finding facts, and rendering awards. To a great extent this board replaced the regular courts as the agency of law primarily concerned with industrial accidents. The judicial system was not entirely supplanted however. Appeals to the regular courts to review the awards made by the Industrial Commission were allowed, but only upon the grounds that (1) the commission acted in excess of its powers, (2) the award was procured by fraud, or (3) the findings did not support the award.[13]

The Workmen's Compensation Act shifted to employers the first impact of a large portion of the expense and loss connected with industrial injuries. Employers promptly shifted the risk of these expenses to insurance companies and all, or almost all, the cost of insurance premiums to the consuming public. The legislation thus created workmen's compensation insurance as a new social institution. By insuring, employers were able to estimate accurately the cost of paying the losses arising from accidents; employees were certain of some basic protection—though this was not in itself assurance that the protection would be adequate; the cost of their injuries was spread over such a large base that no single person or enterprise feared financial calamity due to an occasional serious industrial accident.

Between 1911 and 1913, election to come under the compensation act required affirmative action by the employer. But a 1913 amendment provided that affirmative action by the employer was required to keep him outside the law. Thus employers' inertia was used to extend coverage. By July 1914, 12,500 employers and 250,000 employees were covered; only 607 employers, hiring 5,068 employees, elected to reject the act. These figures include all types of industries, not only mining.[14] After 1911 most of the day-to-day business of settling industrial accident disputes shifted from the courts to the Industrial Commission. Between 1911 and 1956, the commission settled 947,871 cases involving total benefits of $243,397,140, not including cases settled by compromise. Again, these figures concern all industries, not just mining. About 95 per cent of the cases were uncontested and adjustment was reached between the injured employee and the employer, or his insurance carrier, without any formal action being taken by the commission.[15]

The commission—and likewise the courts when their services were employed as reviewing agencies—experienced no great difficulty in administering the act in regard to mining accidents. What difficulty existed in the area of accident compensation, arose in applying the statutory requirement that the accident "grow out of" or be "incidental" to the employment. Much more difficult issues arose when the legislature amended the compensation law to include losses caused by industrial disease. The original 1911 enactment made no specific provision for occupational disease. Thus, for example, it did not cover illness caused by working in polluted air. This lack of coverage was of special importance to the mining industry, in which working places often contained dust, fumes, and gases harmful to human respiratory organs. In 1919 the legislature provided that the compensation law should "include, in addition to accidental injuries, all other injuries growing out of and incidental to the employment."[16]

This terse amendment created problems of the definition of liability. Most of these problems centered on when the claimant was damaged. The time factor was crucial to various issues under the law. For example, the compensation act required that the employee give his employer notice of the injury within a designated period of time after it occurred. The employer at the time of the injury was liable for the payments specified in the act. When the employer carried insurance and changed insurance carriers from time to time, the date of the injury determined which carrier was responsible.

The nature of industrial diseases made it difficult to determine when injury occurred. The time of an accident was easy to determine, for by definition an accident is an instantaneous mishap. When rocks fell upon a miner and broke his leg, there could be no dispute, relevant to the compensation act, about the time he was injured. But such diseases as pneumoconiosis did not result from a single inhalation of mine or factory dust. Long periods of breathing damaging dust particles preceded the onset of pulmonary tuberculosis and chronic bronchitis. Often employees were unaware they were injured until many years elapsed. During the interval between first contact with dusty conditions and manifest injury, the employee might have worked for several employers and might have suffered one or more periods of partial disability. To allocate the employee's economic loss among successive employers in a dusty trade, then, presented a problem of great complexity.

For some years legislation provided no statutory solution. The Industrial Commission and the courts had to contrive their own answers, usually with no precedents to guide them. In an early case following the occupational disease amendment of 1919, the Wisconsin Supreme Court realistically characterized the task which confronted the administrators and the court:

> While occupational disease as well as industrial accident is a part of the expense and ravage of industry, the manner in which disability of the former on the part of the employees is brought about is so inherently different that any attempt to administer the law with respect to one under machinery adapted to the other can but produce botch and patchwork results. However, the administrative officers and the judicial department must strive as best they may with the machinery placed at their disposal, to secure the results which the legislature manifestly intended should be accomplished.[17]

The first case after the 1919 amendment concerned a tool sharpener who suffered disability while employed concurrently by three granite companies. Further to complicate the allocation problem, the three employers contended that before be began work for them the employee had worked for still another employer under conditions which contributed to the disease. The court exonerated the prior employer and held the three current employers liable—assigning to each a portion of the recovery based on the hours worked for each employer.[18] The court freed the prior employer because no authority existed in the law to hold liable a firm not employing the worker at the time he became disabled.

In a 1928 case the court faced a situation where during the period of the claimant's employment the employer had carried insurance with three successive insurance companies. The issue was which of the three insurers was liable for the award. The court held liable the company which was the carrier at the time the worker became disabled, arguing that there was no other practical way to administer the act.[19] To administer the act's provision that the employee give notice of his injuries within thirty days after they occurred, and that the employer provide medical care for ninety days after the "accident," the court felt it necessary to assimilate "disease" to "accident" and to hold that a disease occurred at the instant the worker became disabled.

Using the same criterion as to what event determined the rights and obligations of the parties, the court held in another 1928 opinion that a worker was not entitled to compensation where he became disabled after his employer withdrew from the act.[20] The court deemed it immaterial that for a good many years prior to the employer's withdrawal the employer had consented to the act and that during this consent period his employee inhaled damaging substances. The court felt bound by the act's requirement that the employer be subject to the act at the time the "accident" happened. This same theory was followed in a 1930 case.[21]

Another 1930 case presented a difficult problem of adjusting equities in time. A steel chipper commenced work in 1911 and suffered short periods of disability in 1920, 1921, and 1922. Thereafter he shifted to outside work free from dusty conditions. In 1927 he became totally disabled. In 1929 he died from pulmonary tuberculosis superimposed on pneumoconiosis. Prior to 1926 Zurich General Accident Company was the insurance carrier; thereafter the employer insured with another company. Thus, Zurich was the carrier during all the time dusty working conditions prevailed and also when periods of partial disability occurred; the succeeding carrier was the insurer at the time of total disability. The court refused to hold the second carrier liable for the total damages, since it appeared that the dusty working conditions antedated the time the second carrier assumed liability. A reargument of the case resulted in a redefinition of the holding: "[I]t should be held that the 'time of accident' . . . in cases of occupational disease should be the time when disability first occurs; that the employer in whose employment the injured workman is and the insurance carrier at that time are liable for the total consequences." [22]

This criterion created a gap in the workmen's compensation pattern which the court clearly recognized. A worker who worked under dusty conditions for many years without suffering disability and who then shifted to a healthful job where the disease finally manifested itself was without a remedy under the compensation law, so construed. The former employer was not liable because the act required that to establish a claim the employee be employed by the employer at the "time of the accident." [23] The second employer was not liable since the act required that to found a claim the injury arise out of the employment. The court consoled itself that the number of cases of such unfortunate timing would be small. In any event, it concluded, this was the best the court could do with statutory language designed to compensate for accident rather than disease.

However, in 1932 another case showed that there were still new possibilities of time-sequence problems in this field. A plant employed a granite cutter for many years in work which exposed him to harmful dust. The plant shut down for repairs on December 4, 1928. The employee suffered disability on December 18, 1928, before the plant reopened. He died in April, 1930, and his widow claimed compensation. The employer resisted the award, pointing to the statutory requirement that the worker's injuries must grow out of the employment, and relying upon the prior cases which had determined that the time of the accident for the purpose of the statute was the time when disability first happened. The employer contended that a disability manifesting itself during a shut down could not grow out of the employment because no employment existed at that moment; the argument viewed the case as like that of an employee who broke his leg at home while on vacation. The supreme court refused to accept this brittle logic, which would also deny an award to a worker who became disabled over a weekend, or even after the close of a day's operation. Such an outcome too far denied the benevolent intention of the legislature. However, the court plaintively suggested that it was time that the legislature define its intentions more clearly: "The circumstances under which the employee should be permitted to recover is a matter peculiarly within the field of legislative discretion, and to discover its purpose on this subject we must grope in deep twilight." [24] Out of the twilight the court evolved the rule that the employee might recover if at the "time of the disability the relation of employer and employee existed." If this ill-defined status was present, the employee was protected whether or not he became disabled in action at his workbench.

The inevitably crude time rules worked out in litigation could carry injustice to one side even as they sought a rough equity for the other. A granite cutter worked for an employer for many years. In 1930 a medical examination disclosed a large accumulation of silicosis in his lungs. The employee took a seven-month vacation, after which the first employer refused him further employment. He then took a position with the Kanneberg Company. After thirty-seven and a half days his health again failed. He quit and died less than four months later. The supreme court ruled that the employee suffered a compensable injury in the Kanneberg employment and held that company liable for the full award.[25] Where the second employment contributed to the disability, the employee suffered an injury in that employment within the court's view of the statute, no matter how much of his illness was caused by working conditions in a prior position.

In 1937 the court exonerated the employer of an employee who developed a silicotic condition in the employment, but who suffered no loss of wages—that is, no disability occurred—until after the employer-employee relationship ceased when the employee either obtained another job or retired.[26]

Thus over some fourteen years the cases showed that the court was rarely willing to apportion the cost of industrial disease among consecutive employers, though all contributed to the eventual disability. In the rare case where the employee was made ill while working concurrently for several employers, the court would apportion liability. Furthermore, employees were inadequately protected when they voluntarily left or were discharged from a dusty employment before suffering a disability of any kind.[27]

In 1933 the legislature decreed: "In the case of disease intermittent periods of temporary disability shall create separate claims. . . . '[T]ime of injury' . . . is . . . in the case of disease, the last day at work for the last employer whose employment caused disability." [28] The amendment largely codified prior court decisions and did nothing to relieve some deplorable situations which prior decisions had fostered. A wage loss flowing from inability to work (i.e. disability) was still prerequisite to recovery under the act. Under the decisions and the legislative language codifying them, the responsible employer was the firm employing the worker when he became disabled. When court decisions and the legislative amendment solidified and made certain the above rules, employers governed themselves accordingly. Thus, whenever an employee's medical examination disclosed a serious threat of disability in the near future, the case law and the statutory amendment encouraged employers to discharge the employee.[29] Positions with other employers were closed to such a man; no employer wished to hire one who was soon likely to suffer a wage loss which might establish a compensable claim. An employer who did so, might find himself liable to compensate the employee for a disease having its deeper roots in a prior employment.

In 1935 the legislature tinkered more:

When . . . an employee is discharged from employment because he has a nondisabling silicosis under conditions such as to occasion a wage loss, the commission may allow such sum for compensation on account thereof, as it may deem just, not exceeding seventy per cent of his average annual earnings. Payment of a benefit under this section to an employee shall estop such employee from any further recovery under this section.[30]

Pressure upon the supreme court to construe the law liberally was immense—so great in fact that the court, in a very unusual action, conferred with the Industrial Commission about the problem.[31] Before the 1935 amendment, the basic difficulty was that the statute required the employee to sustain a "disability" before the employer's duty to compensate arose. The legislature had never defined disability. If the occupational disease made the employee ill while at work so that he was unable to return to his job, the case was easy. More difficult cases were those where the employee continued to perform his work, day in and day out, possibly without knowing that the dreaded dust was damaging tissue. If he was then temporarily laid off or fired because of economic conditions or because a medical examination disclosed a health problem, or if he voluntarily retired before the disease rendered him incapable of performing his work, the law did not cover him.

The supreme court ruled, prior to the 1935 amendment, that before an employee could be compensated he had to show that he lacked the physical ability to perform his duties in the usual and customary way.[32] The court recognized that such a holding might require an employee to drag himself to the workroom until he was so physically exhausted that he could not continue. As late as 1935 the court stated: "Unworkable features of the statute have been pointed out in numerous cases, and no one recognizes more than does this court that its clarification is a matter of great difficulty." [33] Clarification, the court decided, was the duty of the legislature. This came in the 1935 amendment.[34]

In 1937 the legislature continued the policy of the 1935 law in a slightly altered form.[35] Any employee, after working for ninety days for an employer under conditions exposing him to inhalation of silica, might claim compensation from that employer. Additional requirements were that the employee suffer a wage loss and either be discharged or voluntarily terminate his employment after the Industrial Commission found that continued employment was inadvisable. The award was such amount as the commission deemed "just, not exceeding thirty-five hundred dollars."

Provisions such as these contained in the 1935 and 1937 amendments prevented employers from discharging employees just prior to disability, in order to escape liability. Furthermore, these amendments encouraged employees threatened with serious illness to shift to healthy but less remunerative positions. Before these amendments, an employee who stopped working in a dusty employment when a medical examination showed that his health was in danger from his current working conditions might be penalized by the move, by losing his compensation claim against the employer who maintained the dusty conditions, since as interpreted by the courts the law prior to 1935 required that in order to establish his claim the employee must be employed at the time disability arose.

Thus the law's handling of the consequences of industrial injuries from 1870 to mid-twentieth century showed great changes in the concepts and agencies employed. The rapidity and extent of these changes were unsurpassed in any other area of the legal history of Wisconsin mining. Old concepts—negligence, contributory negligence, assumption of risk, and the fellow-servant rule—were almost entirely supplanted by new statutory terms—total disability, temporary disability, average annual wage, and injuries growing out of or incidental to the employment. The importance of courts as regulators of human conduct decreased as an administrative agency, the Industrial Commission, took over. Lawyers still found work to do in the area of mining accidents, but the changes wrought in such a short time were remarkable.

In our legal order the legislature holds the principal authority and means to define public policy within the broad framework of constitutional government. Hence, appraisal of the way in which law

meets serious problems in the choice of values, and especially problems generated by major social change, comes to focus mainly on the
legislative operations. In handling the consequences of industrial
accidents in the mining industry, the legislature obviously reacted
with considerable slowness. No special blame attaches to the delay
in bringing under review the concept of fault as a principle of liability
in this field; the problem here was a problem of the whole Wisconsin industrial economy. The common law built on the dominant values of the mid-nineteenth century, which emphasized the increase
of overall productivity and hence protection of capital investment
against law-created risks. Because of the limitations of the times and
the constraints of *stare decisis,* the Wisconsin courts could not alter
the doctrinal patterns well set by the seventies. But like the rest of
the country, Wisconsin experienced a very rapid transition to more
interdependent ways of life in the last quarter of the nineteenth
century. It is understandable that the legislature did not come to
grips sooner with the realities of social and individual costs growing
out of the industrial accident problem, though the lag is enough to
raise the question whether policymaking procedures were not needed
to speed up the investigation of facts and the review of values.

Quite a different judgment must be struck on the poor record of
legislation on the narrower issue of occupational disease. Some fourteen years of litigation and strained decision were here plainly the
product of poor craftsmanship, or the shirking of responsibility, by
the legislature in a field which it had entered but to which it
did not adequately commit itself.

Let us now turn to evidence in the area of prevention of industrial
accidents and disease. What did law do throughout the years to
prevent accidents and disease in the mining industry or to promote
private preventive action?

An 1876 enactment created the Wisconsin State Board of Health
and required mining company physicians to coöperate in gathering
useful information.[36] Terms of this law indicate that the legislature
lacked the detailed information needed to draft adequate safety legislation. In 1883 the legislature created the Bureau of Labor and In-

dustrial Statistics of Wisconsin. Its head, a commissioner, was to collect statistical data covering the commercial, industrial, social, educational, and sanitary condition of laborers. He was empowered to visit factories and to examine the means provided for preventing accidents, to enforce laws governing the employment of minors and females and laws protecting the health and lives of industrial workers. Once again the legislature placed high emphasis upon the duty of the commissioner to gather and report facts. This emphasis reinforces the point just mentioned that a lack of information was a major stumbling block to legislative handling of the problem of mine and factory safety.

Two years later (1885) the legislature authorized the commissioner to appoint one factory inspector.[37] This inspector possessed power to enter factories to investigate compliance with laws regulating safety in working conditions and regulating female and child laborers. The factory inspector filed complaints against violators if they failed to correct unlawful conditions with thirty days after being notified of the defect.

In 1887 the power of the factory inspector extended to condemning unsafe elevators and ordering "bull-wheels, fly-wheels, tumbling-rods, elevator wells, stairways, shafting or dangerous machinery of any kind to be guarded and protected." [38] The statute granted persons injured by condemned elevators a civil suit for damages; it made criminal ($50 fine for each offense) any refusal to guard unsafe machinery.

It is rather interesting to note that with respect to one safety feature, laborers secured protection only after a similar law protected a non-laboring class. In 1871 hotels and inn-keepers were ordered to provide each sleeping room on or above the third story of a hotel or inn with a rope or chain ladder for egress in case of fire.[39] Not until 1878 did the legislature order owners of manufacturing plants to provide their workers with similar protective equipment.[40]

Between the date of the enactments mentioned above and 1911, most legislative efforts were directed toward increasing the efficiency of enforcement and plugging loopholes which appeared from time to time when court decisions determined that the language of some safety enactment did not cover the specific unsafe working condition under attack. Broad language such as is quoted above from the 1887 law ("dangerous machinery of any kind") did not receive a broad judicial construction, and as a consequence amendments outlawing specific unsafe conditions were required.

The number of factory inspectors was increased from time to time, and by 1911 the state had twelve. They met stern resistance from factory owners. One Milwaukee employer tore down the safety laws after they were posted in his establishment. In 1885 the legislature ordered such offending employers fined $50 for each offense.[41]

Enforcement also suffered because before criminal penalties could be imposed a local district attorney had first to file a complaint. In 1887 the legislature ordered local district attorneys to proceed "at once" to file a complaint when notified by a factory inspector that some owner was violating the law. If the local district attorney failed to follow this command, the factory inspector was authorized to ask the governor for the district attorney's "removal for wilful neglect of duty and malfeasance in office." [42]

Before 1900, even if we include all statutes designed to prevent industrial accidents whether they specifically refer to the mining industry or not, the general picture is one of failure to make working conditions safer. This poor nineteenth-century record resulted from several causes. Before the seventies there was little conception of the modern idea of liability, and in the later part of the century there was hostility towards using law to regulate working conditions. For much of the nineteenth-century period there was no organized group to push for reforms. The case-by-case court approach to policy, characteristic of the nineteenth century, served to minimize the important general interests at stake and to obscure the overall success or failure of court-made rules of liability. On the other hand, regulation of the working conditions in even a single industry was almost impossible at the legislative level; the multitude of varying conditions made regulation by a single statute almost a practical impossibility. Legislators lacked the detailed information necessary for comprehensive regulation. Prior to 1900 the legislature had not discovered the usefulness of an administrative agency with fact-finding, rule-making, and supervisory powers. Possibly, the use of the administrative device to regulate working conditions prior to 1900 would have met with judicial disapproval on grounds that the legislature was delegating its power to make laws.

By 1900 it was apparent that the creation of safety rules by direct legislation would not succeed. Between 1909 and 1911 management, laborers' representatives, insurance companies, and the state Bureau of Labor and Industrial Statistics jointly promulgated a set of safety rules covering many dangerous factory conditions. These had no legal sanction behind them, but they were the beginning of safety codes which were soon to come into existence under a 1911 statute. When in 1911 the Wisconsin Legislature created an administrative body, the Wisconsin Industrial Commission, it was vested with power to

have such supervision of every employment and place of business . . . as may be necessary adequately to enforce and administer all laws and all lawful orders requiring such employment and place of employment to be safe, and requiring the protection of the life, health, safety and welfare of every employee in such employment or place of employment and every frequenter of such place of employment.[43]

Mines were included in the term "place of employment," which the law defined as "every place whether indoors or out or under the ground." The law enjoined every employer to furnish "employment which shall be safe for the employees therein," and required further that he "shall furnish and use safety devices and safe parts . . . and do everything necessary to protect the life, health, safety and welfare of . . . employees and frequenters." The commission might investigate and prescribe what means were necessary to make a place safe for workers and frequenters; frequenters included anyone who was not a trespasser. Upon its own motion, or on request of "any person" who suggested that a working place was not safe, the commission might investigate and make any order "necessary to render . . . [the] place of employment safe." Interested parties might test the reasonableness of any commission order in the courts. Ample sanctions existed against those who refused to obey valid commission orders.

After passage of this law, rules governing factory safety conditions took the form of safety codes promulgated by the Industrial Commission. These codes, some general and some aimed at special industries, were formulated in conferences attended by employers, employees' representatives, insurance companies, and representatives from the commission. After this group jointly drafted a proposed code, public hearings were held and the codes often revised to take into account points raised at the public hearings. The codes were then promulgated and given wide public distribution. Safety codes which affect the mining industry were promulgated as follows:

Elevator Code—1913, revised in 1917, 1936, 1944, 1952, 1956.
Mines, General Orders—1913, revised in 1922, 1937, 1953.
Quarries and Pits—1922, revised in 1930, 1933.
Safety, General Orders—1912, revised in 1915, 1932, 1949, 1954.
Tunnel, Caisson and Trench Construction, General Orders—1930, revised in 1936, 1940, 1953.
Explosives, General Orders—1933, revised in 1956.
Fire Prevention, General Orders—1918, revised in 1950.

Beginning in 1917, the Industrial Commission created a safety department to inspect industrial establishments. In 1957 this department employed a mining engineer and two mine and quarry inspectors. These men make inspections to determine compliance with the safety codes.

In 1913 the legislature tied the amount of compensation to the safety law by providing: "Where injury is caused by the failure of the employer to comply with any statute of the state or any lawful order of the industrial commission compensation . . . shall be increased fifteen percent." [44]

The heavy labor of mining attracted few women and children as employees. Thus, although some of the early court cases involved minors employed in less strenuous positions around mines, the problem of female and minor laborers was not a pressing one. In 1889 the legislature ordered that no child under thirteen work in a mine. County judges might grant work permits to children over ten who could read and write English. Violators were fined from $10 to $50, with the money earmarked for schools.

Two years later the legislature stiffened the law. It declared all mine work off-limits for children under twelve and allowed work by children between twelve and fourteen only with a permit. An 1889 law prohibited any person under sixteen from working more than ten hours a day, more than six days a week, or between the hours of 9 P.M. and 6 A.M. In 1903 the age limit below which no child might work in a mine became fourteen; permits might be had for the fourteen–sixteen age group.

Thus, there was a gradual increase of the age limit below which children were not allowed to work in mines. In 1913 the Industrial Commission received power to regulate the working conditions of minors and females. The law declared: "No employer shall employ . . . any minor or any female to work in any place of employment, or at any employment dangerous or prejudicial to the life, health, safety or welfare of such minor, or such female." [45] The act delegated to the Industrial Commission power to regulate the working conditions of females and minors. Until the commission acted the legislature itself provided that certain employments or places of employment should be considered dangerous to the health, safety, and welfare of minors and females. Several of these classifications affected the mining industry. Thus, minors under eighteen were not permitted to work in or about blast furnaces, to run or operate elevators or lifts, to work in any occupation where dust such as emery, rouge, or carborundum was present, or to work in or about any quarry or mine. No female might be employed in or about any mine.

Some remaining laws specifically affecting mine laborers were rather unimportant. Miners' tools were early exempted from creditors' claims. From time to time, statutes made certain that miners would be able to collect their wage claims. For example, an 1889 law decreed that any employee who had wage claims against a mining company for work, labor, or services should have a lien upon the property of the debtor, including all personal property and real property connected with mining. This lien carried a higher priority than any other claim, except taxes. In 1915 a similar lien for wages was granted to laborers working for any firm engaged in quarrying, crushing, cutting, or otherwise preparing stone for any use, or for a firm manufacturing lime.

6

Science and Politics

AMERICAN SOCIETY HAS been influenced greatly by man's success in controlling his physical environment and fashioning it to his ends. Knowledge was prerequisite to control. Law provided the means to acquire the needed knowledge. Even before Meriwether Lewis and William Clark left on their long western trek, government surveyors and explorers had tramped virgin land and the government itself had published reports of their observations. The challenge of vast unexplored territory and the driving urge of hardy settlers to subdue the wilderness bent government and the legal order in the direction of sponsoring explorations and finding facts that would promote settlement. Of all Wisconsin's settlers, the miners were the most impatient and most in need of more information to exploit their situation. An important deposit of a limited natural resource might lie beneath the ground just over the hill. The laggard and the uninformed would miss a fortune.

When miners arrived in Wisconsin, the science of geology was in its infancy. There were few trained geologists in the United States, and they had spent little time in the area west of Lake Michigan. Prior to 1850 there had been only a few surveys of the region. In 1834 the War Department commissioned G. W. Featherstonhaugh to examine an area within the state of Missouri. During that winter he visited the Missouri lead mines and "made a perfectly worthless report." [1] The next year, under the title of United States Geologist Featherstonhaugh explored geological formations in the region between the Missouri and St. Peter (now the Minnesota) rivers. He went on to examine the rock formations of the Wisconsin lead region and assigned them to the carboniferous limestones—a decision which later authority characterized as a "blunder" and "an exhibition of . . . ignorance in the domain of practical geology." [2] Geologist David Dale Owen completed his report (described in Chapter 2) in 1839, but it failed to satisfy the miners. In 1840 a Wisconsin territorial select committee called Owen's group an "army of professed geologists" who just "skinned around"; the committee concluded that little "practical" could be expected to flow from the report. [3] These three feeble attempts constituted the entire survey history of Wisconsin and the immediate region prior to 1850.

Lacking a base of scientific knowledge, miners fell back on practical experience and customary technique. A few contemporary methods could claim some scientific basis. For example, lead miners often dug where they found a certain weed growing; the practice was scientifically sound since the weed grew naturally in a rock formation closely associated with lead ore veins. But other mining practices, such as the use of "tinkembobs" and mediums, had no connection with science.

In view of the lack of, and need for, scientific knowledge about Wisconsin's mineral resources, it would have been surprising had miners not asked for the assistance of the state government. In 1840 the lead region enjoyed a position of great political power. A man from the miners' own area, Colonel Henry Dodge, occupied the governorship. The area held a strong bloc of votes in both houses of the territorial assembly.

As soon as he took office, Governor Dodge urged establishing a state geological survey. He based his suggestion upon the need to aid miners already in Wisconsin and upon the influence the survey would have in bringing immigrants to the state. I. A. Lapham, Wisconsin's first distinguished scientist, wrote the legislature a letter supporting the governor's suggestion. However, the council by an 8 to 5 vote killed a bill establishing a state geological survey. Opposition rested upon the want of funds for the endeavor.

During the territorial period no official governmental survey was authorized. However, there were repeated arguments in favor of such a survey. Thus, in terms typical of the position taken for a survey, on October 10, 1840, the *Madison Argus* urged the economic wisdom of such measures:

After the state government is fully organized, and the state gets free from debt, a wise and beneficent policy will doubtless dictate to our rulers the necessity and propriety of a thorough geological exploration of its surface. . . . As soon as the finances of the state will warrant, we doubt not that this important investigation will be demanded by the general voice of our public spirited and thriving people.

In the absence of a governmental survey, other public and private agencies partly filled the void. Mr. H. A. Tenney collected mineral specimens and deposited them with the state university. A few years later, a university professor of chemistry and natural history was assigned the task of superintending the rather large collection Tenney had amassed. State governors continued to recommend a state-financed survey, but the precarious condition of the treasury stood in the way. In 1852 the state legislature unsuccessfully asked Congress to institute a federal survey, and the state assembly defeated a bill to establish a state survey.

By 1853 several factors combined to create significant pressure to use state funds for geological explorations. By that year many lead mines were worked to water level. Newly invested capital was necessary to explore strata beneath this point. The labor supply dwindled as the western gold fields siphoned off miners. Labor costs increased while production decreased. Wisconsin leaders not directly involved in mining were well aware of the decline in lead production and fondly hoped the industry could regain its former prominence. Congress had refused to intervene, and the industry lacked capital to finance its own survey.

With characteristic underestimation of the task involved, the first state law (1853) authorized the governor to appoint a state geologist and one assistant. The legislature counted on the work of these two men, under an annual appropriation of twenty-five hundred dollars, to complete a geological and mineralogical survey of the entire state. One section of the law ordered that the survey give priority to appraising the lead region.[4]

Governor Farwell selected Edward Daniels to be the first state geologist. In turn, Daniels chose H. A. Tenney to be his assistant. The first report of the new state geologist stated that the work was proceeding diligently with a liberal amount of volunteer assistance. During the first eight months of his appointment, Daniels spent six months in the field. He received free passage on some of the new rail lines in the area. He urged that all persons report production statistics to the survey and deposit mineral specimens with the state university. The state geologist concluded in his first report that the lead mines were at a transitional period. He reported that most of the ore close to the surface was gone and that additional workings would be forced to greater depths. He noted that this fact increased the need for accurate scientific findings to provide an assured base for the industry's future.

Legislators received this report favorably. They were particularly pleased because the state geologist found evidence that lead ore existed in large quantities in the deeper rock formations. A legislative committee reported that several large companies had commenced work in the lead area: the American Mining Company at Sinsinawa Mound and the Mississippi Mining Company at Mineral Point and at Shullsburg. These companies were draining mines by pumps; three other locations were drained by adits. The committee recommended that the state survey be continued.

The serene picture of a state-financed scientific survey—free to conduct its work without governmental interference for reasons of political or economic interest—soon vanished. Within a year after it began, the first survey became embroiled in a struggle for survival and for the right to conduct work and publish reports based on scientific findings. It was a fight that would continue for many years. On January 2, 1854, William A. Barstow, Democrat, succeeded Governor Farwell, Whig. On June 30 of the same year, the new governor peremptorily removed Edward Daniels as state geologist.

This dismissal of Daniels was the prelude to a decade of very stormy relations between the geological survey and the legislature. We must record the broad details of these controversies involving Daniels and several of the men who followed him in the post of state geologist. These disputes are important because issues of fairness to individuals and of efficiency in implementing programs were involved. The detailed attention which the legislature gave these matters was in some sense warranted. However, the most significant feature of these disputes is their irrelevance to the central issue which confronted the legislature in its role concerning the state's mineral wealth. The many battles are therefore important because they cast light upon the character of the contemporary legislative process.

The dismissal of Daniels brought forth accusations from his supporters that the ouster illustrated the spoils system at its worst. Their opponents countered with allegations that Daniels was a "political apothecary" who spent too much time on extra-survey activities. In a more subdued and legalistic vein, Governor Barstow supported his action with two arguments. First, he alleged that Daniels was incompetent and, second, that Daniels' discharge was justified by a provision in the 1849 Revised Statutes which declared: "All officers who are or shall be appointed by the governor for a certain time, or to supply a vacancy, may be removed by him." [5]

The 1855 legislature named a select committee to investigate the discharge. The committee's report sided with Daniels and recommended that the state appropriate nine hundred dollars to pay him for the balance of 1854. The committee found Daniels' work adequate and, in support, cited letters from the Pennsylvania state geologist, the director of the Virginia Survey, and a professor at an eastern college. Without much argument, the committee concluded that the Wisconsin statute did not grant power to remove Daniels.

The bill to appropriate funds to pay Daniels provoked a second complete investigation in the same 1855 session by the judiciary committee of the assembly. The result was a majority report supporting the previous select committee. The majority observed that the survey could not function if every change in the party controlling the governorship was followed by a change in the head of the survey. The section in the Revised Statutes did not apply because it covered "employments" but not "offices." The minority report urged that a rapid turnover in the post of head geologist was not harmful: "It is not at all probable that any one man will be able fully to complete the survey of our state." [6]

Daniels' pay bill failed by a close assembly vote of 39 to 31. In 1857 the legislature approved a bill awarding him $312.50; the sum represented payment of his salary up to the time when he received word of his dismissal. Thus ended the first chapter of the history of the survey.

Governor Barstow appointed a strange individual to replace Daniels. The character and eccentricities of James Gates Percival directly colored chapter two of the survey story. Percival was a learned man, and his learning extended to many areas other than geology. He wrote poetry in thirteen languages; in his day he was regarded as the peer of the poet Bryant. He was a self-taught philologist, and he was conversant with most Continental literature, which he read in the original. Before coming to Wisconsin, Percival assisted Noah Webster with his dictionary. To fill the state job, Barstow induced Percival to leave more remunerative employment with the American Mining Company in the lead district.

Percival devoted himself to intellectual pursuits so diligently and intently that he neglected his dress, his living habits, and his money matters.

He walked with his head bent, his eyes cast downward, and with slow and uncertain step. Those of our citizens who often saw him will not soon forget his aspect of poverty, almost of squalor—tattered gray coat, his patched pants—the repairs of his own hands—and his weather-beaten glazed cap, with earpieces of sheepskin, the wooly side in.[7]

These and other queer living habits made Percival a most unusual man. But it was his lackadaisical stewardship of his personal finances which affected the geological survey he headed. He had no desire to accumulate a fortune. He lived from hand to mouth, spending money as it came to him, and did not worry about the source of future funds. When he obtained money, he used it to increase his large personal library.

Percival assumed his duties almost immediately upon his appointment. Two reports, one published posthumously, detailed his labors. Both were heavy scientific documents lacking in sharp or picturesque description and filled with minute observations derived from slow, careful search. Many pages contained detailed maps and drawings of mineral ranges and rock formations.

The reports were the kind to delight professional geologists. However, they failed to excite lead-region miners. The miners wanted to know where ore could be found. The prime question to which the legislature and the lead region wanted an answer was, What were the ore possibilities in the deeper rock formations, particularly in the lower magnesian limestone? One of Percival's reports stated:

On this point, of so much importance to the mining interest, I had then ascertained a series of facts which seemed to prove that all the limestones, from the surface of the upper magnesian . . . [Galena limestone] to a considerable depth, at least, in the lower magnesian, were good lead-bearing rocks.[8]

Whether Percival would have found a basis later to strengthen this tentative conclusion was never revealed. On May 2, 1856, Percival died suddenly, after serving a little over twenty-one months as state geologist.

A serious dispute over the handling of state funds followed Percival's death. Percival's administrator, Dr. J. L. Jencks, informed state officials that he doubted whether Percival had received all sums due him. This claim soon erupted into a major battle involving the honesty and truthfulness of the state's chief executive. In 1857 Jencks' claim on behalf of Percival's estate went before a joint investigation committee. During his lifetime Percival received payments directly from the state treasury. The committee called upon Barstow, who by this time was no longer governor, to produce vouchers showing the amount he had paid to Percival. Barstow's cryptic reply arrived after

Jencks had left Madison. Barstow submitted no vouchers, but concluded that the state owed Percival's estate $1,160. The 1857 legislature appropriated $1,635 for the estate.

When the 1857 legislature adjourned, it left behind a joint committee to investigate the departments of state government. This committee soon heard reports that Jencks was dissatisfied with the settlement. Also, rumors circulated that shortly before he died Percival lacked enough funds to care for himself properly. Rather gratuitously the committee assigned itself the task of doing "justice and honor to the state."

The committee quickly disposed of the main issue by finding that the state was not "properly liable for any greater sum" than that already paid Jencks. The committee regretted that Percival had died embittered against the state believing himself "defrauded of the dues he had earned" and the victim of "ingratitude, neglect and practical repudiation." Accepting this as Percival's state of mind just before death came, the committee apportioned fault for Percival's feeling between Barstow and Percival himself. The committee felt that Percival was to blame for suffering in silence when, "had his wants been more generally known, his wrongs would have been promptly remedied at the hands of the legislature." Barstow was made out to be a villain in the affair. He had withdrawn all of the appropriation from the state treasury; in fact, the account was overdrawn. Some five months after Percival's death, Barstow returned $1,760 to the state treasury to be credited to the survey account.

Unwilling to let matters stand in this posture, the assembly of the next legislature referred the joint investigation committee report to a select committee to "report such facts . . . as they shall deem proper." This select committee procured all of the vouchers. The resulting majority and minority reports both left far behind the main issue of how much money the state owed Percival. Instead, ex-Governor Barstow became the central issue. The majority report found that Percival's bitterness was directed against Daniels supporters who had tried to unseat Percival. Furthermore, it concluded that Percival felt no ill will towards Barstow. It referred to a letter

Barstow wrote Percival a few months before Percival's death, stating that funds would not be withheld because of delay in completing a report. The majority ignored the fact that this letter was written after a resident of Hazel Green begged that Percival's salary be sent to him because he desperately needed it. Although Percival's reports lacked a poetical touch, the majority report of the investigation committee did not, as the following excerpt will show:

[D]uring his last sickness everything was done that human skill could device [*sic.*] Every comfort was provided, and his every wish anticipated and gratified. He was surrounded by those who had learned to appreciate the society of a man from whose lips fell thoughts clothed with the drapery of virtue, wisdom and innocence, often sparkling with gems of pure and lofty sentiment, gently dripping like the silvery streamlet glistening in the sunlight as it trickles down the mountain side.[9]

Assemblyman James Baker of Walworth County decided that it was "incumbent on him to expose the fallacies and absurdities of the remarkable whitewashing report of the majority." He blamed the failure to settle the whole matter earlier upon Barstow's failure to supply the vouchers. Baker wrote that past criticism of Barstow was "moderate in . . . [its] strictures" and no amount of "garbling and perverting the evidence of witnesses" could hide the plain fact that wrongs were committed against Percival at a time when he was suffering from want.[10]

The unfortunate thing about the Daniels and Percival affairs was that they were irrelevant to more fundamental issues which should have been pressed in the legislative arena. The real public issues were: Was the state government acquiring reliable and realistic data on the mineral resources available for the growth of Wisconsin's economy? What was the proper balance between the honest search for reliable information and the desires of particular interests to affect that search for private gain? What use should be made of law to regulate and foster the healthy growth of the state's mineral potential? To these important issues the legislatures gave scant and limited attention. The enormous amount of legislative time spent upon the hiring, firing, and performance of state geologists, even after Percival's death, as will be seen presently, is evidence of the legislature's lack of self-discipline or sense of professional approach to its primary job—making broad policy decisions. The legislature seemed willing to devote its time to episodic, limited, personalized controversy, especially if there was some partisan tinge to be given to the particular matter. While legislative time was thus frittered away, more basic policy decisions remained undecided.

When by 1858 the last investigation had run its course, Jencks was able to secure an additional $350 for Percival's estate. One might suppose that hostility to the survey would accompany these disputes, but it did not. Only one bill was introduced to abolish the survey (1855), and it never came to final vote. In 1857 Governor Bashford told the legislature that lead production increased because of "more scientific and thorough modes in working the mines." [11] And in 1857 a committee praised Percival's incomplete report. At Percival's death only four months of his term remained, and for that time the post of state geologist remained vacant.

Shortly before his death Percival informed the legislature that "the advantage of a survey conducted by one person, is the systematic unity which such can best give the whole." [12] Almost in open defiance of this warning, the legislature, in 1857, established a third survey headed by a triumvirate: James Hall of New York, and Ezra Carr and Edward Daniels of Wisconsin. Daniels was the former state geologist; Carr was a doctor of medicine and a professor of chemistry at the University of Wisconsin; Hall was an eminent geologist, burdened at the time with work as state geologist for Iowa and with geological work in Canada.

Even before the law was passed, letters between Carr in Wisconsin and Hall in New York foretold an intra-survey squabble. Carr urged that Hall assume the directorship; Hall demurred upon the ground that Daniels was a candidate for the position and that Hall's support was pledged to him. Ten days after the law was published Carr wrote Hall that the governor and Carr desired Hall to head the team. The letter continued: "The Governor understands Daniels and said to me that you and myself, being a majority, could arrange matters." [13]

The 1857 law appropriated $6,000 per year for the work of the survey and provided that the compensation for each commissioner should not exceed $2,000 per year. The law was vague about whether any one of the three men might draw $2,000 per year for salary plus an additional sum for expenses. To the extent that anyone drew expenses in addition to the $2,000 yearly salary, the amount remaining to pay the salary of the other two was reduced because only $6,000 a year was appropriated to cover all salaries and expenses of the survey, exclusive of printing costs.

Shortly after the Bill was passed in March, 1857, Daniels met Hall in New York. These two had no trouble in apportioning the survey duties among the three men. Hall was unable to come to Madison immediately, and Daniels reported the conference to Carr and Governor Bashford. When Hall did arrive in Madison in April, 1857, Daniels was in Kansas. Hall and Carr agreed that each commissioner should have one-third of the annual $6,000 appropriation—and no more. Upon Daniels' return Carr informed him of this agreement. Hall had meanwhile returned to New York. Daniels objected that this was not the law's intent.

The survey statute required that each commissioner execute a written contract with the state. Governor Bashford engaged a Madison attorney, J. C. Hopkins, to draft the contracts. The drafts granted each commissioner the right to draw $2,000 per year as payment for personal services "together with the expenses incurred by him for necessary assistants, room rents, and the other expenses incurred by him in the discharge of his duty." [14]

On June 19, 1857, Carr and Daniels agreed to come to the attorney's office and sign these documents. The governor affixed his signature and left before the two arrived. Daniels signed his and left before Carr arrived. Carr refused to sign, and Hall later did likewise. Daniels began work; the other two did not.

Immediately after convening, the 1858 legislature requested information about the argument. Governor Randall replied that Daniels alone was working and had expended $2,017.19. All three men wrote the legislature, explaining their respective positions. Daniels submitted a report of his work, and an assembly select committee seemed favorably impressed. A bill to repeal the survey appeared but mustered only scattered backing. There was more support for another bill which replaced the old survey with a new one. This new bill contained provisions defining the handling of expenses (thus covering the Daniels-Hall-Carr dispute) and prohibiting withdrawal of survey funds except upon "proper verification of accounts" (to prevent another Percival-Barstow incident).

The contract already signed by Daniels now became troublesome. What rights existed between Daniels and the state? That issue and the proposed bill were referred to a select committee, which immediately proceeded to investigate the entire Daniels-Carr-Hall feud.

The committee reached no agreement. A majority construed the prior law to apportion the $6,000 annual appropriation three equal ways. Daniels' contract was declared "utterly void," and the majority recommended that the survey be abolished. The minority viewed the results of Daniels' work as more important than a "discussion of the legal questions involved," and proposed that the survey be continued under Daniels' leadership but with a less generous appropriation.

The 1858 session did nothing to the survey. One bill died in committee; one was indefinitely postponed; and one was laid on the table by a close vote of 39 to 31.

Two weeks after the 1858 legislature adjourned, the three survey heads called off their feud, signed new contracts, and began work. The position of Hall and Carr prevailed: the new contracts awarded each man $2,000, *including* his expenses.

For the next several years the survey scene was peaceful. Only occasional criticisms appeared, usually directed against the fact that the survey lacked a single head. In 1859 the governor reported that the survey was hampered by this defect and by the lack of "concert and harmony between the commissioners." The legislature requested opinions from any of the men "present in the city." The request produced a report from Carr on behalf of himself and Hall which was conspicuously silent about Daniels. The three men filed separate formal reports for that year.

In 1860 the governor said that the survey had made good progress, but suggested that the legislature investigate the survey as a "justice to the Commissioners and their assistants" in order to silence criticism in some quarters. The ensuing investigation generally approved the work done but concluded that "the efficiency of the survey has been impaired by the want of a responsible head." The committee found no "unity of design, harmony of action and self-sacrificing devotion to science" such as it thought the state had a right to expect. The 1860 legislature enacted several changes recommended by its investigating committee. The most important change was that the new statute designated Hall to be head of the survey.

In 1861 the legislature appropriated $3,000 to publish one thousand copies of a report on the lead district written by a survey assistant, J. D. Whitney. This appropriation amounted to a striking vote of confidence, because the state was extremely short of money and was involved in war at the time. Other survey manuscripts did not fair so well. Hall failed to obtain money to publish his work on paleontology. Daniels' manuscript was judged not of "sufficient importance" to publish. Two bills to abolish the survey failed by pocket veto, and a joint committee was created to examine the entire program.

The most important act of the 1861 session was a resolution passed near the end of the session:

The Governor is hereby directed to withhold any further order on the treasury to James Hall, Ezra Carr and Edward Daniels, with whom contract has been made for a Geological Survey of this State; and the Governor is hereby requested to take all lawful and proper means to annul said contracts, and suspend any further survey and expenditure therewith.[15]

This directive placed the governor in a dilemma. He doubted his power to annul the contracts, which had several years to run. The legislature adjourned without taking up the governor's suggestion that the direction be made by statute rather than by resolution, to give it "as much force as the act authorizing the contracts."

At the next session (1862) bills to abolish the survey appeared in both houses. A senate committee reflected legislative feelings when it labeled the survey a failure. The intent had been, said the committee, that a "respectable volume" would be published each year, but state expenditures of $30,000 had produced only one publishable manuscript, and that was not yet available to the public. The strength of the critical attitude may be assessed by remembering that from Daniels' first term down to Hall's, annual survey reports were submitted to the legislature. The committee report failed to mention these annual reports.

That the 1862 committee should assess the survey a "failure" is understandable only by noting the purpose the legislature had in mind for the survey. Legislators fondly expected to receive optimistic survey reports which would exalt the soil resources of Wisconsin, help sell state lands, settle the state by drawing new settlers, and foster industrial growth by enticing investment in Wisconsin economic enterprises. No less than a glowing, comprehensive final report, published for all the world to read, would achieve these ends. Cautiously factual reports buried in annual volumes containing several scores of other state documents did not satisfy the legislators' promotional ambitions.

Several other occurrences at about the same time created more ill will for the survey. First, one of Hall's assistants asked for an additional $4,500 to finish some work. Second, publication of the one volume on the lead district was overdue. At the session's beginning, the governor informed the legislature that publication would be delayed until about February 1. Hall even came to Madison to explain the delay. The book did not appear in February, and the legislature passed two resolutions to look into the matter. Finally, on March 27, a legislative committee reported that the books were at the Madison depot—held for unpaid freight charges.

The 1862 legislature abolished the survey. By resolution it requested the governor to notify the three survey commissioners that their offices were forfeited for neglect of duty. The same resolution asked the attorney general to ascertain if funds already paid to the commissioners might be recovered.

Daniels and Carr stopped work immediately. Now discharged

twice as a Wisconsin state geologist, Daniels retired from the scene. Carr soon migrated to California where he later became state superintendent of public instruction. Hall felt enough personal hurt to demand an investigation. Favorable action upon this request resulted in a legislative report which cleared him of blame. The report blamed Daniels for "hogging" the appropriations during the survey's first year. In an attempt to silence criticism of Hall, the report found that Hall had returned all specimens belonging to the state, except a few that he was still studying.

For thirteen years more, Hall and the Wisconsin legislature feuded over trivia. Hall wrote letters to the governor and to the legislature detailing his efforts in Wisconsin. He seemed more interested in getting his Wisconsin work published and in repairing damage to his reputation than in pressing the legal argument that the state had broken a contract by dismissing him. On the other hand, the legislature persisted in the belief that Hall had retained specimens rightfully belonging to the state. As late as 1875 Hall sent a memorial to the legislature. No more of the survey's work was ever published at state expense. No more money or specimens ever changed hands. Hall printed his work on paleontology elsewhere; Charles Whittlesey, a survey assistant, did likewise with his material on the Penokee mineral range. Ironically, Whittlesey's report was later reprinted, at state expense, in a publication of a later Wisconsin survey. Thus ended this unhappy chapter of Wisconsin survey history.

Legislative dissatisfaction rested on more than disgust over the survey's household squabbles and shock over irregular management of survey appropriations. These defects were quickly investigated and remedied by amendatory acts. The basic, although unarticulated, disappointment rested upon the legislature's displeasure with the slow pace of survey work and the content of the geologists' findings. To the legislature, the survey's purposes were to inspire capital investments in a faltering lead industry and to demonstrate the mineral wealth of the entire state so as to nurture the growth and settlement of Wisconsin.

Highly significant evidence of the legislative aims for the survey is the fact that a legislative committee praised the initial geological report issued by the first state geologist, Daniels, for the "practical" matters in it. In 1853 a senate committee recommended that the state finance geological work because it could eliminate much of the uncertainty in the search for ore. Money and time spent by persons without adequate data was unproductive. The committee agreed that this was a "problem which should be solved by the state government." Almost always messages of the state chief executive urging the institution or continuance of survey work mentioned the argument that the survey would nourish a supply of capital for mining endeavors.

These ends could be achieved only by highly favorable and widely circulated publications. It was also essential that these reports be written by skilled and impartial geologists. One legislative desire—that the survey rapidly complete an examination of the entire state—remained far from fulfilled. This desire flowed naturally from mid-nineteenth-century thinking, which placed first emphasis upon speedy economic development. But the legislators persistently underestimated the magnitude of the task they set the survey.

The best example of the kind of survey findings which legislators and mining men deplored was Whitney's opinion of the lead district in the volume published with the legislature's authorization. With the caution of a careful student, Whitney reported:

[We] are not prepared to admit that the Lower Magnesian ever has been, or is likely to be, profitably mined in for lead even when it comes to the surface, or when it is overlaid with other rocks. . . . [We] are able to affirm that, at the present time, no profitable mining is carried on in the Lower Magnesian, and that none ever has been for any length of time; and, farther, that no well-developed crevices, or such as could be found to any distance, have ever been found in it.[16]

After the legislature abolished the survey, the problem remained of disposing of the 1,000 copies of the Whitney report. No doubt many wished them abandoned to the railroad for the freight charges or locked in a basement room of the Statehouse, but such was not their fate. The bulk of the edition, 947 copies, was distributed to legislators and other public bodies or officials. This left 53 copies in the governor's hands, subject to legislative disposal.

The supply did not meet the demand. Governor Salomon could not fill numerous requests for the book. Bills to permit the governor to distribute the remaining books and to give them to the legislators from the three lead counties met defeat. Official records do not disclose the fate of the books. A movement to reprint the book was beaten down with the argument that reprinting was "inexpedient."

Experience with the first two surveys dampened enthusiasm but did not cause all public officials to give up completely. Almost before the ink on the repeal bill had dried, the legislature requested the governor to submit the annual reports. The governor complied but justified his action of not submitting the reports before the request by pointing out that legislative abolition of the survey occurred before the governor had received the reports.

Two years later (1864) Governor Lewis' annual message urged consideration of a new survey. Lewis based his recommendations on the industry's need for capital and on the aid a survey could furnish in encouraging the entry of capital. In the lead region, drainage projects were needed for exploiting mines below flood levels. But such drainage required capital well beyond the ability of individual proprietors to supply. For example, about 1870 one owner drove a tunnel one mile long at a cost of $80,000; in 1876 a cloudburst filled it and almost destroyed its value.

The Civil War and its aftermath postponed serious consideration of the issue until 1869. That year Governor Fairchild's annual message reopened discussion of the subject:

A thorough geological survey of this state is much needed. Could we present to the world a scientific and comprehensive account of our vast mineral and agricultural resources, it would draw hither within a few years, millions of dollars of capital for investments. In such an investigation of her hidden sources of wealth, Wisconsin is far behind the neighboring states of the Northwest.[17]

In 1870 Fairchild repeated his urging, and an assembly committee seconded his suggestion. The committee was most concerned over the decline in lead production, which had gone to 12,500 tons yearly by 1870, as compared to an average annual output of over 21,000 tons during the decade 1841–51. In 1870 the legislature authorized and "requir[ed]" the governor to appoint one commissioner to survey that part of the state "known as the 'lead region.'" The law authorized four assistants, established a daily wage for all, including the commissioner, and required the commissioner to subscribe an oath of office and post a $5,000 bond.[18] In a contemporary report, the Wisconsin State Agricultural Society articulated the motives for this law:

This important act originated in a strong desire on the part of a large number of intelligent people of the lead district, for a more careful and full examination into the reasons which induced Prof. J. D. Whitney, of the late Geological Commission, to discourage the hope of making deep mining successful.

. . . [G]reat interest is felt in . . . [a forthcoming report], which it is understood will warrant at least in part a reversal of the judgment pronounced in 1860.[19]

Six days after signing the act, the governor appointed John Murrish to the commissioner's position. Murrish understood the needs of the lead mining area, for he had served his apprenticeship in the mines of Cornwall. Murrish went to work immediately and by January, 1871, he had placed his first report in the governor's hands. Even before the report was published, rumors spread that its contents would undo some of the damage of the pessimistic Whitney report.

At the climax of his document, Murrish approached the most important question: the richness of the deeper rock strata. The report stated that north of the Wisconsin River in Richland County (i.e., outside the lead region), Murrish found "good specimens of lead ore . . . equal to anything we find in the lead district proper." Further, he said:

It is true these deposits in the Lower Magnesian, out of the lead district, do not compare with the very heavy deposits of ore in the upper Magnesian in the lead district, and it would be unjust to draw a comparison between them, from the fact that the same evidences of the action of physical forces from beneath are not found. Yet when compared with similar places in the Upper Magnesian out of the lead districts, under similar conditions, the lead bearing qualities of the Lower Magnesian are equally apparent.[20]

On the important question—the degree of promise for further mining developments—the report was something of a mystery to all its readers, from public officials to lead-region miners. The report was not optimistic about the lower magnesian, as the miners had hoped; neither was it pessimistic, as the miners had feared. The governor quickly consulted with a committee of the legislature, and it was agreed that Murrish should devote more time to the question. Thus the policy-makers thrust Murrish squarely into the fire.

In January, 1872, Murrish filed a report devoted almost entirely to the issue of the richness of the lower magnesian. The preface demonstrated that Murrish knew his precarious position. He wrote that doubt concerning the lower formations was "certainly one of the most important questions concerning our mining interests in the lead district, one upon which the future of these interests must depend." [21] The report, however, carried no prediction about answers to the vital questions. The supply of zinc in the formation between the upper and lower magnesian was enough to "last (with our present force of mining) for the next century." Mining men were not interested in zinc—nor in keeping the work force at its "present" size. In his only comment on the Whitney report, Murrish said merely that he did not entirely agree with its conclusions.

The importance of Murrish's work in the lead region was that he refused to be drawn into making conclusions which were beyond the knowledge of geologists. Murrish stated his factual findings in simple language and then stopped. He quietly refused to predict the richness of the lower magnesian formation. This did not satisfy lead-region miners. It did, however, establish a standard of scientific freedom for such survey work, which came to full bloom or expression a decade later under a subsequent survey. Henceforth, the state's survey officers would freely report facts which they discovered, and let mining entrepreneurs and investors draw their own conclusions.

Some dissatisfaction with Murrish's tactics manifested itself in several bills to repeal the survey, but other forces prevented their passage. In 1859 an assembly resolution had recited that all land north of 45 degrees latitude (approximately a line from St. Paul to a point thirty-five miles north of Green Bay) had interests more in common with those of the Upper Peninsula of Michigan, and that these two areas should form a new state. The 1859 resolution proposed to consent to the formation of a new territory (the Territory of Superior), provided Michigan agreed. Michigan did not agree, and the plan died. By 1870 the lack of interest in northern Wisconsin which prompted this resolution had completely disappeared. Enterprising and hopeful Wisconsin had "discovered" its northern part, and new interest in the north's unexplored mineral wealth worked against bills to repeal the geological survey. Accordingly, in 1872 the legislature extended the Murrish survey northward from the lead district on a line running to the "intersection of the Penoka [sic] or other iron ranges" and including all "mineral deposits of an ironomic value."

Murrish remained survey head one year more. During that time he examined iron ore possibilities around Baraboo, Sauk County, then struck northward toward Wisconsin Rapids, went on to Black River Falls and back to Stevens Point, and then concluded with a "hasty" trip to Wausau. Murrish's third report detailed findings made on these trips. He wrote that from Wausau to Lake Superior there was "unbroken forest, unexplored and comparatively unknown" where any geologist would have to "take his pack on his back, and make up his mind to live in the woods, away from the borders, even of civilization." [22]

Murrish's efforts after finishing in the lead region were general explorations rather than detailed examinations. His final report aroused interest in the mineral potential of areas outside the lead district. He found "float" iron ore in Sauk and Richland counties, porcelain clay near Wisconsin Rapids, and some poor magnetic iron ore around Black River Falls. In keeping with his refusal to make predictions, he cautioned: "In their undeveloped condition no man can form a correct estimate of the extent or value of these ore districts. . . . Nature, as a general thing, gives only on the surface the indications, with a few illustrative specimens, of her richer deposits that lie beneath the surface. These indications I have furnished, . . . the specimens I have placed in the museum. And from these things I hope every one interested will form his own opinion." [23]

Against this background, Governor Washburn, early in 1873, began pushing for a more extensive survey. He argued that Murrish's findings had already caused some excitement and warranted a more thorough survey. The legislature responded by repealing all existing survey laws and providing for a "complete geological, mineralogical and agricultural survey of the state." [24] The lead region shared the attention of the survey with the northern part of the state. The 1873 act required that work begin in Ashland and Douglas counties, but it stipulated also that there be a careful topographical survey of the lead region.

The legislature provided that the new survey be organized under a single head. On April 10, 1873, Governor Washburn appointed increase A. Lapham to the post. This choice was excellent, for Lapham was rightfully regarded as the state's peerless man of science of his time. The law also authorized four subordinates, and the men chosen for these positions proved to be excellent men of science and fine public servants. Roland D. Irving was a professor of geology at the University of Wisconsin and a graduate of the Columbia College School of Mines; T. C. Chamberlin was a professor of geology at Beloit College, who later became president of the University of Wisconsin (1887–92); Moses Strong, son of the former United States District Attorney, was a Yale graduate with training on the Continent; W. W. Daniells was engaged as the survey's chemist. The University of Wisconsin permitted gratuitous use of the school's facilities.

The bond thus early established between the state university and the new survey proved mutually beneficial and grew stronger throughout the years. That the survey staff included an important number of men with university tenure implied the freedom from political and industry control which Murrish originated. The survey staff, young in years (Chamberlin, thirty years old; Strong, twenty-seven; and Irving, twenty-six) brought to their work youthful energy and adequate geological training, both theoretical and practical.

To detail all the field work accomplished and to describe the published results of this new survey would outreach the scope of this essay. The original staff and the more than twenty others associated with the survey at one time or another in its following fruitful years, produced the most thorough and complete survey of resources ever made in so short a time. The comprehensiveness of their work is illustrated by the staff force in 1876 which included an ichthyologist, an ethnologist, and an ornithologist. In contrast to the earlier surveys, this survey suffered no criticism of the devotion of its staff or the quality of its documents.[25]

Three parties, each headed by a survey assistant, did most of the field work. Irving's team explored the iron and copper ranges in Ashland and Douglas counties in 1873, then the Penokee range and areas around Black River Falls; in 1874 they explored from Dane County northward to Wausau. Chamberlin's party explored southeastern Wisconsin. Strong assumed responsibility for the lead region and areas northward across the Wisconsin River. Railroads furnished free transportation for men, equipment, and specimens.

The initial legislation authorized a four-year life for the new survey, to expire in 1877. In 1877 the legislature extended the period to five years, and in 1878 the period was extended to March 31, 1879, with the provision that the staff might work beyond that date, if necessary, to prepare and publish the final report. An 1879 act authorized payment of a "fair and just compensation" to survey members who chose to work beyond the expiration date.

Prior surveys had been plagued by two problems. First, there had been bickering among survey personnel and executive interference basically motivated by political considerations. Second, popular dissatisfaction had followed the publication of unpopular survey results. In smaller measure the new survey encountered like troubles.

Lapham's 1873 appointment as survey head occurred too late to be submitted to the senate for confirmation. Had the regular course of proceedings been followed, the appointment would have been submitted to the next session. The survey statute required that the selection be "with the advice and consent of the Senate." For reasons which the record leaves unexplained, the appointment was not submitted to the senate. No one complained in 1874, but in 1875 a senate resolution asked the senate judiciary committee to report whether there was a "legally qualified state geologist." Lapham's death rendered the issue moot and Governor Taylor submitted the name of O. W. Wight as the next head.

Dr. Wight later noted that his nomination was confirmed with "singular unanimity".[26] However, all survey assistants quickly tendered their resignations to Wight. Later all the staff, except Daniells, reconsidered and stayed with the survey. We have different accounts of what was back of these moves. According to Wight:

> The assistant geologists, following a rule of courtesy under such circumstances, offered to surrender their commissions. The newly appointed chief . . . [Wight] requested them to withdraw their resignations, and to continue their work. With this request they cheerfully complied. The resignation of Prof. Daniells, however as chemist to the survey was accepted after due deliberation.[27]

The story had another cast, as contained in a letter from Irving to Hall in February, 1875, the same month Wight was named survey chief:

> Our geological survey has gone the fate of its predecessors—or rather a worse one. The governor has appointed a disreputable politician to Dr. Lapham's position, leaving the survey still unorganized. We had accomplished an immense amount of work. . . . It is probable that none of it will ever see light. . . . Wisconsin has most certainly had ill luck with her surveys.[28]

In addition to Irving's appraisal, other evidence indicates the political nature of Wight's appointment. Lapham was appointed by Governor Washburn, a Republican; Wight by Governor Taylor, a Democrat. Wight resigned forty-four days after Governor Taylor was replaced by Governor Ludington, a Republican. Even after

Wight's tenure ceased, some hard feelings remained. For example, Wight refused to coöperate with his successor, Chamberlin, in preparing the final report. Chamberlin decided to place in the final report the 1873, 1874, and 1875 annual reports because they had not been printed when submitted. After deciding to eliminate parts dealing with administrative details, Chamberlin asked Lapham's son to edit the 1873 and 1874 reports written by his father. Chamberlin tendered a like courtesy to Wight, who had written the 1875 report. Wight declined to do the editing, and Chamberlin did it himself. Wight did read the proofs, and he assured Chamberlin that nothing valuable was omitted.

The other difficulty familiar from the course of other surveys was the unpopularity—or at least disappointment—attending some reports. This factor appeared in connection with two areas surveyed under the new project set up in 1873. Early in the life of the survey, Irving had explored the Penokee iron range. His report was not as optimistic as many interested parties wished. Irving suggested to Hall shortly after Wight's appointment that part of the unease manifest at the time arose because of "my refusal to call the Penokee ores so rich as Col Whittlesey [a staff member of a preceding Wisconsin survey] makes them to be." [29] Chamberlin later added more facts. He praised Irving and wrote in a national publication in 1889 that the scientist in his Penokee study encountered

unwarranted expectations raised by previous flattering opinions respecting the richness of the iron deposits given by incautious and inexpert explorers. His perfectly candid and unreserved report brought the usual reward of frankness and sincerity in the face of opposing desire, at first a storm of protest and of adverse criticism, which even threatened the existence of the survey, later, a sullen acquiescence in the truth, and finally, an admiration for the correctness and the courage of the position taken and the diversion of enterprise from unprofitable into successful lines of exploitation. [30]

Shortly after his appointment, Wight borrowed E. T. Sweet from Irving's field staff and headed north to re-explore the Penokee range. Wight stated that the trip's purpose was to make a "more careful and accurate geological section of Penokee Mountain." In his sub-

sequent report Wight stated he was "less reserved . . . in express-
ing an opinion as to the value of the iron deposits in the Penokee
range." The Penokee range and its value was of paramount importance in the 1870's, since in 1872 iron had been found there.
Many promoters were busy after that, forming companies, selling
stock, and mining ores. Obviously, individuals interested in Penokee
development were concerned with what the geological survey reported about the area.

What the survey reported concerning the richness of the lead
region's lower magnesian formation also failed to please many interested parties. At the beginning of the survey Lapham had formulated a policy of freedom for his assistants. For example, his first
report stated:

> It is perhaps to be regretted, that the necessity of extending the geologi-
> cal survey over the whole state . . . renders it impossible to make such
> special surveys of each mining district as are wanted for the practical
> purposes of the miner, and seem to be expected in some localities. Such
> working plans can only be made by the mining companies and landed
> proprietors. Had this work been undertaken for each mining neighbor-
> hood, there would have been but little time or means left for the prose-
> cution of the survey in other portions of the state.
>
> .   .   .   .
>
> It is the proper business of the miner, at the expense of the owners, and
> not of the geologist at the public expense, to search with pick in hand, . . .
> for mineral ranges, sinking shafts here and there until he meets with
> success. . . . Surveys and plans are necessary for the proper working of
> any mines, as has often been found at great cost; but they do not come
> within the requirements of the law authorizing and defining the present
> geological survey of Wisconsin.[31]

Lapham's second report reiterated these views.

> Wherever mining has been prosecuted in search of gold, silver, copper,
> etc., examination of the rocks gave little indication of the presence of
> these metals; and it has very often been the business of the survey to dis-
> courage the search for ores in places where they are not to be found.[32]

The difficult task of exploring and reporting conditions in the
lead region fell to Moses Strong. In Lapham's second annual report

he courageously tackled the still explosive question of the district's richness.

Mr. Strong's survey, and the experience of the past twelve years have given additional proof of the correctness of the views of Prof. J. D. Whitney, as set forth in his report, published in 1861. Among the more important of these views are the following:

.   .   .   .

That though the mineral grounds have considerable lateral extent, they reach only a short distance downwards.[33]

This remained all that the survey published about the issue until the appearance of the final report. Moses Strong contributed a little over one hundred pages to the final report. On the issue of the region's future, Strong noted,

I have been obliged to omit . . . the much argued question of mining in the Lower Magnesian limestone. No discussion of this question can do it justice which does not take into consideration the origin of the crevices. . . .

The discussion of this question would have occupied more space in the report than I felt justified in devoting to theoretical questions, at the expense of what appeared to me to be important practical facts.[34]

Whether by choice or by accident the task of predicting the future of the region fell to Chamberlin. Chamberlin said that he assumed the task because of "Mr. Strong's preference." This suggests that Strong deferred to Chamberlin because discussion of a question which might produce repercussions affecting the very life of the survey properly belongs to the chief and not to a subordinate. At any rate, Chamberlin devoted another two hundred pages of the final report to the lead region.

Chamberlin squarely faced the issue. He believed that theories about the origin of the lead deposits would give an answer to the possibility of ore in the lower strata. He rejected all previous theories that the lead was left by heated vapor or hot water rising from deep within the earth. His theory was that in the far geological past, when Wisconsin was covered by water, lead was carried by strong oceanic currents until positioned over the lead district. There some unidentified "precipitating agent" caused the currents to drop their heavy burden. From this theory Chamberlin deduced his conclusions.

> The long mooted question of the probabilities of probable deep mining in the lead district presents itself for foremost consideration. . . . It is a matter of supreme practical and theoretical interest to determine whether the formulations lying below are productive or barren.
>
> .   .   .   .
>
> [W]e arrive at the general conclusion . . . that the deposits in the Lower Magnesian limestone beneath the productive deposits of the lead region would not be found as rich as the latter.
>
> .   .   .   .
>
> [It] is quite improbable that mining in the Lower Magnesian limestone could be practically profitable.[35]

At the time Chamberlin wrote these unenthusiastic words about the lead region (1877), miners were conditioned to such pessimistic opinions, and no furor resulted. In fact, Chamberlin believed that miners had come to appreciate dismal reports. "The people have, however, generally recognized the fact that it is more important to know the truth than to be beguiled into useless expenditures by a flattering hypothesis." [36]

The final report was more reserved about the lack of northern copper deposits. It found that at least $100,000 had not been "judiciously" expended due to a lack of information about a "proper system of mining." The guarded conclusion was: "Although none of the mining enterprises have proven successful they do not demonstrate, by any means, that valuable deposits of native copper do not exist in the district." [37]

The original survey law contained no provisions for printing survey reports. When the field work neared completion, attention turned to publication. Men in charge of the survey contemplated from the beginning that a "final" report would follow completion of the field work. In 1875 Moses Strong reminded the legislature of Lapham's original intention to publish two volumes as a final report. The Wisconsin Teachers' Association urged that the design of plates in the final report be such that a simple school text could be prepared from them.

In 1876 the legislature directed the preparation and publication of the final report. It directed that one part of the report be written in "clear, plain language, with explanations of technical terms" and devoted to the "general geology and the leading facts and principles relating to the mineral resources of the state, together with practical suggestions as to the methods of detecting and utilizing the same, so as to constitute the material for a volume suited to the wants of explorers, miners, landowners, and manufacturers, . . . and to the needs of schools of the state." [38]

The legislation did not describe the rest of the report, evidently assuming it would be more technical than the part for which specifications were given. The law authorized 7,000 copies of the "practical" part and 2,500 copies of the rest. Lengthy provisions covered the report's distribution. Schools, judges, libraries, legislators, learned societies, and designated state officials were beneficiaries.

Four substantial volumes resulted. Volume I was published last (1883) because it drew upon material contained in the other three. Volume II appeared in 1877, Volume III in 1880, and Volume IV in 1882. The appearance of these volumes concluded the Lapham-Chamberlin survey.

What might be called the "last" geological survey appeared in 1897. The method by which this survey came into being and the scope of its activities bear marked evidence of the fact that the survey no longer served only the mining industry. In 1893 the Wisconsin Academy of Sciences, Arts and Letters established a committee to secure legislation authorizing a new survey. One year later the committee reported; in 1895 a bill was introduced but defeated; the year 1897 brought success. [39]

General management of the new survey was vested in the five ex officio members of a commission, consisting of the governor, the state superintendent of public instruction, the president of the University of Wisconsin, the president of the Wisconsin Academy of Sciences, Arts and Letters, and the president of the Commission of Fisheries. Detailed supervision rested in a superintendent appointed by the five commissioners. The total annual appropriation provided was only $5,000. Thus, even though the law limited the five commissioners to expenses, it was apparent that if the survey was to cover much territory, many of its workers must be content to receive no more than reimbursement for expenses and possible publication of their research.

The specific areas of work outlined in the law show a broadening of survey activities to matters outside those of immediate concern to mining and minerals.

1. Completion of the geological survey of the state, especially a survey of the iron ores, building stones and road building materials.

2. A study of the soils of the state.

3. A study of the plants of the state with special emphasis upon trees and conservation.

4. A study of animal life and fish.

5. A completion of the topographical mapping of the state.

6. A preparation of manuals for school use.

Other areas of work assigned to the survey after it was created were not of major interest to the mining industry, but were of great benefit to the state as a whole, and perhaps also of incidental value to the mining industry. In 1907 the legislature authorized the survey to test and recommend road construction materials. The survey organized a highway division which besides dealing with plans, specifications, and materials also conducted many meetings designed to educate the public about the need for, and the problems involved in, a public highway system. Although the creation of a highway commission in 1911 took from the survey many of these responsibilities, the survey continued for many years to coöperate with the highway commission in locating local road-building materials.

Beginning in 1905 and for over forty-five years thereafter, the survey devoted much time to surveying the surface water resources of Wisconsin. This work included locating and determining the extent of the available water power, gauging the flow of streams, and studying the effects of drainage upon the volume in water courses.

In 1945 survey exploration of underground water resources commenced. Thereafter much work in this area was accomplished by federal and state coöperation. From 1909 on, soil investigation and soil mapping became a survey function. From 1911 until 1934 topographic mapping work was a survey responsibility. Finally, the survey assisted in efforts to find a workable method of assessing mineral lands for taxation.

This brief recital of activities in non-mineral areas shows that the survey performed many services for other segments of the economy. But the mineral interests were not ignored. The original 1897 enactment specifically mentioned a survey of the iron ore resources. In 1903 the legislature directed that special attention be paid to clay resources and the lead district.[40] In 1907 the lead and zinc region was again specifically mentioned.[41] Iron ores and fluxing limestones were segregated for preferential attention in 1911, and in 1949 a separate appropriation was made to survey the "mineral resources of the state." [42]

This chapter has followed several problems common to all of the surveys. One of the important issues was the struggle to allow the surveys to investigate and report, impartially, facts about the mineral potentialities of several areas of the state. Even after fifty-four years' experience, this difficulty recurred.

Around 1900 public interest in the old southwest lead district revived. Motivated by this show of interest, the survey detailed Professor Ulysses Sherman Grant of Northwestern University to study the region, especially diggings which had been opened or extended since Chamberlin's report issued some twenty years previously. Grant outlined his purpose as a statement of the present and future possibilities of mining lead and zinc. In 1903, a year after completing the field work, Grant published a "preliminary" report. The major part covered strictly geological data and facts discovered in the field research. However, he did reach the question that had gone unanswered through the years.

And this brings us to another important question, and that is whether mining . . . can be carried on profitably at any considerable distance below the separation between the Trenton and the Galena. To this question the writer is able to give no definite and precise answer . . . It can be stated, however, with a considerable degree of certainty that no deposits of importance are to be expected in the St. Peter sandstone, while for deposits in the underlying Lower Magnesian limestone the same statements can be made as have been made for the Trenton.[43]

The 1906 "final" report stated:

Considerable attention has been devoted by the miner . . . to the question of prospecting for ore in the Lower Magnesian formation. In regard to this matter it may be stated, that some ore has been found in that formation . . . but the ore bodies . . . are not anywhere nearly as extensive as those which occur in the Galena and Platteville, and it is doubtful whether ore deposits of economic value exist in the Lower Magnesian.[44]

Grant further stated that exploration in the lower magnesian would be very expensive, and the report as a whole left a clear impression that miners and mining companies would be better advised to spend time and money searching for lead and zinc in strata above the lower magnesian. The report painted a rather dismal picture of most mining efforts in the area. Grant found that mining was conducted in the same "primitive manner that it . . . [had] been for years past." There was much off-season mining by farmers, no use of steam, compressed air, or electricity for drilling, and many diggings were still not explored or had not been worked below water level.

The record gives no indication that Grant suffered criticism because of his conclusions. By 1906 lead-region interests were conditioned to pessimistic reports about the richness of the lower magnesian. No large number of people had great expectations which Grant's report could disappoint. This was not true of the other mineral area of which Grant wrote.

Almost at the same time that lead interest warmed, northern Wisconsin copper attracted attention. Activity first centered in the Upper Peninsula of Michigan and soon spread to contiguous northern Wisconsin. The survey sent Grant to examine two areas: the Douglas range in northern Douglas County, and the St. Croix range in southern Douglas County. Simultaneously with the formulation of survey plans in the St. Croix region, promoters launched a new company, the St. Croix Copper Company of Lake Superior. An elaborate preliminary prospectus described the company, its $1,500,000 capitalization, and the prospects that northern copper possessed. Shares sold for one dollar each. Mr. Ernest A. Arnold, a lawyer from West Superior, was vitally interested in the new company. He and others in the area welcomed survey field men in the summer of 1899. Grant and Arnold got along very well throughout the field research. Grant reported later that the people of Douglas County showed "cordial interest . . . in the work of the Survey" and that Mr. Arnold "generously placed his knowledge of the county and a considerable part of his time at the disposal of the Survey." [45]

Recognizing the immense public interest in the area, the survey published a preliminary report of the investigation. The publication, appearing in 1900, stated: "As far as the results of the exploration which has been carried on thus far . . . were open to inspection of the Survey, it can be stated that in no place was a deposit of copper, which was of sufficient richness, shown to be of any great extent." [46]

Although a careful reading of the entire report disclosed that the conclusion was a "preliminary" one, a few individuals blew up a storm of criticism. E. A. Birge, survey director, and C. R. Van Hise, consulting geologist, received critical comments, especially from Mr. Arnold. Legislative representatives from the area joined in these protests. Some threatened that survey funds would be cut because of the report. Several attackers suggested the work be re-done under a different survey employee.

Survey heads backed Grant, who in turn issued a second report. The same findings, with some exceptions to be shortly mentioned, were printed. Van Hise attached a note saying that the report did not attempt to predict whether Wisconsin possessed copper deposits of economic significance. The second report stated that the first report did not indicate that there were no Douglas County copper deposits.

[N]o such statement was made,—nor is any such statement made in this edition of the report,—and such an interpretation does not seem to be justifiable.[47]

The second report reiterated survey policy in the following language:

[A] state geological survey . . . should discuss, in a calm and unprejudiced manner, the conditions which are favorable and those which are not so favorable. . . . The position of a state survey . . . is exactly that of an individual who has been intrusted to make a report on a given property. He would be untrue to his trust should he fail to state the facts which were favorable to the property . . . , and he would be just as untrue should he present only the favorable side . . . and leave untouched the side which might not be so favorable.[48]

An appendix to the second publication reported that Mr. Arnold and others had caused blasting to be done at four places on the St. Croix range, and had reported good results. However, readers were told, the survey had not examined the new work.

Gradually through the years the geological survey carved out for itself a role of protecting several interests from unwarranted mineral exploration. Individual investors and the public generally interested in the judicious use of men, machinery, and capital, were furnished a measure of protection by the survey. With the passage of time, this role came to be accepted as a proper survey function, though no statute ever articulated it. In 1929 the survey sponsored a pamphlet on "The Negligible Oil and Gas Possibilities of Wisconsin." The publication frankly stated its purpose to be a review of the scientific evidence supporting a general conclusion that there was little likelihood of finding oil or gas of commercial quantity in the state. One cannot help speculating what would have followed the appearance of such a report about the time the oil boom of 1865 was getting under way.

The mining industry reaped considerable benefit from a by-product of survey work, the valuing of mineral lands for taxation. For many years, as will be pointed out in the following chapter, Wisconsin tax collectors struggled with the difficulties of applying an ad valorem tax to mineral properties. In 1913 the legislature ordered the survey to assist by examining northern mineral land to ascertain ore potentialities. The legislature hoped that the survey would produce data from which a reasonable value might be determined for each mineral property. The irregular area covered was in Ashland, Bayfield, Washburn, Chippewa, Rusk, Sawyer, Price, and Oneida counties. In 1913 and 1914 the survey examined almost 2,500,000 acres. The result, published in 1915,[49] stated that one objective of the study was to promote "the prevention of waste of money and effort . . . by pointing out the most favorable places for exploration, and thus concentrating the attention of explorers . . . where . . . most likely to be successful." The report covered most of the area by townships. Even before it was published, it was made available to the public in Madison. Many individuals and companies examined the report as a basis for exploration. By 1928 and 1929 so much interest in the report was manifested that a new edition was published.

The survey's growing freedom from identification with the mineral industry may be seen in some changes effected in its institutional organization. In 1931 survey ties with the University of Wisconsin strengthened when the Board of Regents was empowered to appoint the state geologist and to direct survey activities. In 1953 the separate appropriation for the survey, which had appeared in every legislative session since the turn of the century, disappeared. Thereafter, survey funds became a budgetary matter for the state university, and the state geologist became a regular member of the University faculty.

The public benefit involved in expenditures for geological surveys in Wisconsin rested on a broader base than additions to the sum of theoretical knowledge. At mid-twentieth century, expenditures solely to increase human theoretical knowledge recommended themselves to many policy makers because the relationship between theoretical and practical had been demonstrated so often that the existence and force of the connection was admitted. One hundred years before, in 1850 for example, lawmakers certainly would not have established a geological survey in Wisconsin if proponents had pointed only to the advance of human knowledge. However, the practical benefits of a survey were many, and policy makers in the 1850's were never asked to justify survey appropriations solely by theoretical benefits.

Mining interests which initially led the fight wanted a state survey for one purely practical reason. They conceived the task of the survey to lie in pinpointing rich mineral areas which could be privately developed. But beyond this very pragmatic argument were other practical benefits from a survey. Wise policy planning in the field of legal regulation of a limited natural resource demanded facts about the resource to be regulated. The solution of social problems, such as unemployment and industrial accidents and diseases, required facts which a survey could provide. And last, but certainly in no sense least, decisions about the type and amount of the mining industry's contribution to the expenses of government in the form of taxes could not be made without knowledge of many facts of the industry.

The difficulties which beset many of the Wisconsin surveys resulted from conflicts among these practical reasons for the surveys' existence. Mining interests demanded quick and optimistic results, whereas legislators needed complete and accurate facts from the surveys if they were to make wise, beneficial, and lasting laws. Serving these two aims at the same time was impossible. When survey administrators chose to work slowly and accurately, the wrath of mining interests descended upon them. But survey heads and their subordinates chose usually to make careful examinations and to follow these with completely candid reports, although they did not have the backing of any statutory language guaranteeing them and their co-workers the right to use state funds in the pursuit of truth in this manner. To their credit, they did so anyway, and in the long run the state profited more from their efforts than if they had followed the path desired by the mineral interests.

7

The Public's Share

THE IMPORTANCE OF the history of taxing Wisconsin's mineral wealth lies deeper than a recital of statistics showing the total tax burden imposed by the lawmakers throughout the years. Of greater import are the successes and failures of various taxing techniques used, the legal and practical problems encountered, and the general philosophy behind the taxing schemes selected.

Probably the sole function of most taxes is to raise revenue to pay the expenses of government. This is what Justice Holmes pointed to when he said: "Taxes are what we pay for civilized society." [1]

Professor Friedmann states another possible function of taxes: "Taxation is one of the most important weapons by which the State can mitigate the two objectionable aspects of private property; firstly, the inequalities of wealth, and secondly, the power to use private property for private purpose, and without regard to community purposes." [2] Thus, taxes may be used as regulatory instruments; the revenue produced may be incidental. Regulatory taxes may operate in two general ways. First, heavy tax duties hinder or abolish undesired activities. Second, light tax burdens encourage desired activities. Whichever regulatory route is followed, lawmakers find their objective more easily secured if they have leeway to draw distinctions and to impose different levies on various businesses, properties, or activities.

Through most of Wisconsin's history the backbone of its taxation system was a general ad valorem property tax—a tax levied against owners of property based upon a value assigned to their real estate and chattels. The most important features in the history of mineral taxation lie in administrative difficulties of applying the ad valorem property tax to minerals, and in legislative deviations from this norm.

Prior to statehood, scant attention was paid to the taxation of lead, the only mineral of any importance at that time. The Congress did not levy a general ad valorem property tax upon mineral land. Congressional policy was to encourage settlement of the West and a tax on ownership of real estate of any kind would have hampered this aim. Furthermore, certainly in theory, the United States owned almost all Wisconsin lead deposits prior to about 1845, and nothing was to be gained by taxing property owned by the government. Congress attempted to gather revenue from the lead lands through leasing and licensing miners and smelters. As seen in a previous chapter, the net return from this venture was small and contributed very little to federal government expenses.

During territorial days a territorial statute levied taxes upon "all lands, town lots, and out lots, which are not exempted from taxation by the laws of the United States, or this territory, and not including any improvements made thereon." [3] There is no evidence to indicate that under this law any large taxable real estate value was assigned to land because of its mineral deposits.

When statehood arrived, government costs forced Wisconsin lawmakers to search for revenue to operate the state. Indeed, opponents of statehood had argued that these governmental costs would be so burdensome that continued territorial status with accompanying federal appropriations was preferable. To meet the revenue demands of the new state, chapter 15 of the Revised Statutes of 1849 provided for taxing all real and personal property not exempt from taxation. Section 2 defined real property to include land, buildings and other fixtures and improvements, and "all mines, minerals, quarries, and fossils in and under the same." Thus, unlike the territory, the state expressly declared mines and minerals to be taxable.

This ad valorem property tax required valuation of the property taxed. The 1849 law directed the assessor to accept the value which an owner ascribed to his real and personal property if (1), as to personal property, the owner at "any time before the assessor shall have completed his assessment" made an affidavit setting a value, and (2), as to real estate, the owner valued it by an affidavit signed by himself and by "a disinterested freeholder of the same town or ward, not of kin."[4]

Since land values change from time to time and are governed by many variables, no way exists to conclude whether mineral lands were overvalued or undervalued as compared to other property during most of Wisconsin's history. One might suppose that no overvaluation occurred under the 1849 law which vested valuation power in the owner-taxpayer. At no time in the history of Wisconsin does there seem to be public record of great, wholesale protests against unduly high mineral-lands valuations.

Throughout the nineteenth century, the tax on real estate values remained. Legislatures made changes from time to time in the statutes relating to the mechanics of finding the land's value. In 1868 the tax law directed assessors to value the land "from actual view at full value."[5] Assessors were directed to consider the "mines, minerals, quarries or other valuable deposits known to be available therein." In 1877 the duty to assess upon actual view was limited to towns containing 108 square miles or less.[6] In 1878 the duty was limited to towns 48 square miles or less in area.[7] Finally, the duty to assess only upon actual view was eliminated altogether. The progressive decrease in the size of towns where actual view was prerequisite to valuation coincided with the expansion of settlement into the difficult and thinly settled northern areas of the state.

Throughout the nineteenth century legislative declarations clearly expressed the lawmakers' intent that mineral deposits should be considered in valuing land. The following language was typical: "In determining the value the assessor shall consider, as to each piece, its advantage or disadvantage of location, quality of soil, quality of standing timber, water privileges, mines, minerals, quarries, or other valuable deposits *known to be available therein, . . .* and their value. [Italics added]." [8]

The thought behind the injunction to consider "known" deposits is obscure. No reported court opinion ever threw light upon its meaning. When did an assessor "know" that land contained mineral deposits? How convincing should the evidence be before he could "know" this fact? This legislative language grew out of a physical difference between underground mineral wealth and aboveground factors which affected land values. Trees and buildings were visible. This is not to say that timber valuation was easy. The extent of the timber, its quality, and many other factors presented factual questions and broad issues of judgment. Mineral wealth, on the other hand, was not visible. Many deposits were not even known to exist, and the known existence of some commercial ore provided no guide concerning its extent or its richness beyond the area of immediate exploration.

In one sense the statutory stress on "known" deposits was superfluous. It directed an assessor to tax the value of ore only if he knew it existed. One is prompted to ask, How could an assessor tax ore that he did not know was present? The legislature probably covered two ideas by the quoted language. First, it wanted it known that mineral deposits were taxable. In other words, the language made certain that lands rich with known deposits of ore were not to be valued as if minerals were absent. Second, the legislature employed the quoted language to guard against unwarranted mineral valuations based on flimsy evidence or mere suspicion. There is some evidence that assessors were occasionally overzealous and overoptimistic, and sometimes in certain areas of the state assigned a large value to land based upon an unproved assumption that it possessed great deposits of minerals. Valuable discoveries in the general neighborhood frequently induced assessors to speculate that all the surrounding land was richly underlaid with deposits. When we remember the sanguine reports and predictions in nineteenth-century newspapers, and even in public documents, concerning the mineral wealth of the state, we can well appreciate that the legislature was concerned that only "known" deposits affect land values.

The nineteenth-century ad valorem taxation of mineral wealth was impossible to administer. One qualified authority so characterized the job: "It is recognized that it is impossible to determine the true value of a mineral deposit in advance of its complete exhaustion." [9] It must be remembered, too, that for the greatest part of the nineteenth century the science of geology was not well developed; in particular, knowledge about Wisconsin's rock formations was scant. The nature of the problem would not yield to legislative fiat. Effective taxation must wait upon knowledge.

For a good many years, local assessors struggled to value mineral lands. Most of their efforts resulted in guesses. These men lacked the knowledge, the facts, and the time needed to do better. In the twentieth century legislatures sought more scientific mineral-land valuations by requiring that the state geologist and the State Tax Commission assist by recommending values to the local officials.[10] A 1941 survey concluded that local officials "usually . . . [raised] the state valuations." Despite this trend, Wisconsin mineral lands were not taxed as heavily as those in adjoining states. For example, in 1914 the State Geological Survey reported with respect to valuations in southwestern Wisconsin: "Inspection of the assessment rolls has shown, however, that as a general rule very little increase assessment has been placed upon mineral lands in the past on account of its mineral content. A few cases have come to light, on the other hand, where strikingly excessive valuations have been placed by local assessors upon certain mining properties." [11]

In mineral taxation the style of tax levy may induce mining practices which bear closely on waste or conservation of the natural resource involved. Experts feel that an ad valorem property tax may retard extensive exploration to ascertain the extent of a given deposit. Since an ad valorem tax is an annual levy upon the value of minerals known to be underground, owners and lessees hesitate to gather proof of the extent of their holdings. If deposits are charted years in advance of their extraction, knowledge of their presence will increase the land's value each year until the minerals are removed. Geologists point out that wasteful practices may result from the owner's ignorance of the nature, location, and extent of the entire ore body. If such wasteful mining techniques occurred in Wisconsin, there is no public record of it. The lack of interest in conservation is demonstrated by the absence of any argument against the ad valorem tax based on the point that it might tend toward wasteful mining.

An ad valorem tax may influence owners in a second direction contrary to good conservation. The annual tax based on value induces lessees and owners to "mine from under the tax." Under this tax pressure owners and lessees seek to subtract ores quickly and to take first high grade ore and ore most easily mined. Their plan is to decrease the land's value as quickly as possible—preferably before the next annual tax day appears. In so far as mining from under the tax runs counter to a mining plan designed to secure all the commercial grade ore in the ground, conservation of natural resources suffers. There is no public record to show that in Wisconsin there was felt widespread inducement toward wasteful operations of this nature, but, again, the relation of the methods of taxation and conservation was never adverted to by public authorities. No public body ever investigated the interrelationship of taxes and conservation. Particularly in the nineteenth century, legislatures lacked interest in conservation and in the use of taxation as a regulatory devise.

It is possible that considerable mining from under the tax occurred. This possibility is supported by evidence in another area of activity where a levy analogous to a tax induced improper mining techniques. In the zinc region after 1900—and quite possibly before —fee owners commonly leased their land to mining companies for a flat royalty per ton of ore mined. In 1911 the Wisconsin Conservation Commission pointed out that this situation encouraged some lessees to mine only the high grade ore. They left in the ground low grade ore which cost more per ton of refined metal to produce.

The low grade ore was left because it required the same royalty payment to the lessor as a ton of high grade ore. The commission reported that "in the zinc district closer mining is done in the case of those companies who own the fee than by those operating on the lease system." [12] Here, then, was an instance where mining from under a royalty influenced mining practices and resulted in loss of usable ore.

The ad valorem property tax presented one administrative difficulty which remained unsolved at mid-twentieth century. Property law permitted owners of land to grant leases of underground minerals and allowed separate ownership, with one person owning the surface property and another the sub-surface resources. Applying the ad valorem tax to this system of separate property rights created problems which were outlined by Judge Arthur Kopp of Wisconsin's Fifth Circuit. Judge Kopp, who was familiar with the problem from a generation of law practice in the lead and zinc area, took an active part in the attempt to legislate away the difficulties:

Shortly before the turn of the century geologists became interested in the formations in southwestern Wisconsin and contended that under these shallow deposits of lead ore would be found large valuable deposits of lead and zinc. As a consequence, every man who had had any mining on his land considered that his particular farm was one on which there would be an "Eldorado." And so the practice grew by which the grantors when they sold a farm would reserve the "mineral rights" or "the rights to mine for lead and zinc" or some other general language attempting to reserve to the grantors the right to, at some future time, enter the premises and mine the same. Up to that time, there was no way under the law of taxing this reserved title to "mineral rights" and so the value of the supposed ore deposits was assessed to the owner of the fee. . . . About this time mining became very exciting. . . . As a consequence, if a discovery was made on A's farm the taxing authorities concluded that B's farm adjoining it must also have ore under it and shot up the assessments sometimes tremendously. This of course became very burdensome to the owner of the general fee. He had no way of protecting himself. The mineral rights were conveyed from one to another and, it was an encumbrance upon the farm so that the farmer wanting to sell his farm would have difficulty in getting rid of it.[13]

Prior to 1903 the law collected from the owner of the surface estate all taxes, including any amount based on the part of the valuation attributed to minerals beneath the surface. As long as the mineral estate was not considered valuable by either the assessor or the general public, the surface owner did not complain. But when the mineral estate became valuable according to public opinion, the surface owner found himself paying taxes on someone else's property. Moreover, he was embarrassed when prospective purchasers objected to the surface owner's inability to convey the mineral estate.

In 1903 the legislature provided that the surface owner might request that the assessor assess the mineral estate separately. Thereafter, the mineral estate owner owed the tax on his property, and the separate mineral estate might be foreclosed for nonpayment.

This law did nothing to clear land titles by revesting the mineral estate in the surface owner. As Judge Kopp states:

This did not cure the situation. Owners would convey the mineral rights to others and when it came to selling them no one had any way of knowing whether they were worth five cents or five million, and so someone would buy the mineral rights for a nominal amount and still the farmer would have an encumbrance on his title.[14]

In 1913 another law provided that if the owner of the mineral estate suffered his holdings to be sold for nonpayment of the taxes, only the surface owner or the state might bid at the foreclosure sale. If the state purchased the mineral estate, the law granted the surface owner a three-year period within which to buy the mineral interest. Otherwise the law prohibited the state from selling the mineral rights. The intent of the law, Judge Kopp notes, was "to give the farmer opportunity to buy in the encumbrance against his property or force the owner thereof to pay the taxes on it."

Owners of valuable underground mineral estates would pay taxes assessed upon their holdings. Owners who reserved minerals only because of custom or because of a flimsy hope that the land contained mineral deposits would be unwilling to pay taxes upon estates of highly doubtful value. The intent of the law was that eventually the latter estates would be foreclosed for nonpayment and that the mineral title would be reunited with the surface estate.

In 1915 the Wisconsin Supreme Court declared the statute unconstitutional, as violating the equal protection clauses of both the Wisconsin and the Federal constitutions.[15] The vice was that the treatment established for foreclosure of mineral estates differed from the tax foreclosure procedures for other kinds of property. When non-mineral property was sold, any person might bid at the judicial sale, but the 1913 law permitted only the state or the surface owner to bid when mineral property was sold for nonpayment of taxes.

By mid-twentieth century this same problem plagued titles to many acres in northern Wisconsin. Many sellers, often long prior to 1950, had sold large quantities of land, reserving mineral estates. By 1950 owners of these reserved mineral estates were often the heirs of the original vendor. Many times the heirs were numerous and even unknown. Frequently public authorities foreclosed tax liens upon the land and then discovered a lack of bidder interest at the tax sale because uncertainty existed about whether the title obtained at the sale included the mineral estate. Often the land's value rested almost entirely upon the hope that minerals were present. The uncertainty surrounding the issue cooled bidding at tax sales and decreased public revenues. Furthermore, the ownership of the reserved mineral estate was fractionalized among many widespread heirs of the person who had originally reserved the minerals. This made it almost impossible for any large mining company to acquire good title to the mineral estate. Consequently, development of the mineral potential of the area lagged.

In 1953 a bill proposed to clear away the uncertainty by providing that the "estate vested in the grantee of any tax deed . . . shall include all minerals and other valuable deposits in such land, and the right to enter and remove such minerals and deposits, to the exclusion of any person who may have formerly owned any such rights." [16] This bill failed to secure assembly approval.

There were possible approaches other than the ad valorem tax, to taxing minerals. Throughout the nineteenth century, and indeed up to 1927, as it affected mineral land taxes, the Wisconsin constitution provided that "the rule of taxation shall be uniform"; but despite this command, attempts were made prior to 1927 to provide a different taxation method for mineral lands. In 1859 an unsuccessful bill proposed to exempt for six years the property of individuals or companies making iron and zinc from native ores. The bill defined "property" to include veins of ore. In 1887 a bill which failed to pass would have provided a special tax of $2 for each $1,000 of capital stock of every mining company in the state. In 1913 the senate indefinitely postponed a special mining tax bill. In 1923 a special iron-mining tax bill was withdrawn by the author.

Some of the efforts produced laws. In 1877 the legislature directed that assessors value iron-mining properties without considering the value of minerals. To the value thus obtained, assessors were ordered to add the net value of ore taken from the ground during the year immediately preceding the date of the assessment. This value then became the assessed value of the property to which the general property tax levy was applied. At the time the bill was passed there were doubts about its constitutionality, probably because the law established a non-uniform method of taxing mineral properties. The law was dropped during the 1878 revision of the state statutes. The revisors indicated that they struck out the provision because of doubts about its constitutionality.

An 1883 law exempted from state taxation all property of any corporation or association engaged in the manufacture of oxide of zinc or metallic zinc from native Wisconsin ores. The exemption period was for three years. For many years state officials had been conscious of the fact that most Wisconsin zinc ore was refined in Illinois. For example, in 1873 Governor Washburn told the lawmakers that he hoped they could find means to encourage the manufacture of zinc in the state in order that native zinc would contribute its part to the state's economy.

A 1915 statute provided that the value of lead and zinc mines should be computed by adding to the value of the land, determined without considering the fact that it contained minerals, one-fifth of the gross proceeds of minerals sold during the preceding year. The history of this statute indicates that its passage was sought by lead- and zinc-land owners to protect themselves from high assessments imposed by local assessors who sought to estimate the value of underground deposits. In 1953 the statute was extended to all mineral lands except those with iron ore. Thus, by 1953 the valuation of mineral lands, with the exception of iron-rich areas, depended upon past factors which could be established with certainty. Valuations based upon the unknown, and unknowable, quantity and quality of underground mineral wealth disappeared.

Prior to 1927 all these proposed bills and enactments ran a grave risk of being declared unconstitutional because they applied to mineral lands a method of taxation different from that applied to other real property. In 1911 the governor focused public attention upon mineral-land taxation. Governor McGovern pointed out that timber lands were taxed every year at full value because timber was visible. His opinion was that underground mineral wealth was not taxed because its existence was often unknown to the taxing authorities. Minerals brought to the surface, he informed the lawmakers, were immediately shipped outside the state and beyond the state's taxing power. He suggested taxing minerals when they were brought to the surface. In 1913 he repeated his suggestions, and pointed out that many lumber companies had sold timber lands after removing the trees and in the conveyance had reserved title to the underground mineral estates. These reserved mineral estates were not taxed at all, according to the governor.

The culmination of this movement started by Governor McGovern was a 1927 amendment to the state constitution which permitted the legislature to provide different taxes for forests and mineral lands. The amendment added the words that I have italicized to the constitution: "The rule of taxation shall be uniform, and taxes shall be levied upon such property *with such classification as to forests and minerals, including or separate or severed from the land,* as the legislature shall prescribe. [Italics added.]" [17]

Subsequent to the 1927 constitutional amendment, many bills

proposed special tax rules for mining properties and businesses. A 1941 proposal to levy ten cents upon each ton of iron ore produced failed. In 1943 a proposal for such a tax upon companies in operation ten years or more was defeated. In 1947 the senate adjourned without taking action upon a joint resolution which sought to establish a committee to investigate the feasibility of levying a tax on iron ore. Proponents supporting the study argued that adjoining states received considerable revenue from such taxes and that mining communities were entitled to levy such a duty to compensate themselves for the "waste" and disturbed and disorderly landscape left by mining operations.

Two proposals made after 1927 were enacted. They provided good examples of twentieth-century use of taxing power as a molding or regulatory device. In 1947 persons or associations owning "lead and zinc mines, or mills finishing the products of lead and zinc mines or the smelters" were granted a special depletion allowance or deduction from their gross income in arriving at net income for purposes of the state income tax law. The allowance was on a sliding scale varying from 15 per cent on the first $100,000 of gross income from ore sales, down to 3 per cent of sales over $300,000. The law required that the income-tax savings attributable to this special deduction from gross income should "be used by the taxpayer in prospecting for ore, and proof thereof duly verified shall be furnished the tax commission." The obvious intent of the statute was to encourage prospecting by requiring the tax savings to be used in that field.

In 1953 the legislature enacted a tax law applicable to low-grade iron ore properties. Low-grade iron ore was defined as ore that could not be marketed in its natural state and that required fine grinding in order to render it usable. Generally, the law established a special tax that took the place of the ordinary real and personal property taxes which would otherwise be applied to low-grade properties. The property exempt from the ordinary taxes and subject to the special tax included not only the iron mine itself but other property used in the refining process, such as the buildings housing the grinding equipment, tailing basins, stripping dumps, and transportation facilities. The tax rate specified was less while the plant was under construction. After construction was completed, the amount of the special tax depended upon the output of the plant.

The purpose of the statute was to encourage the building and operation of low-grade iron ore plants. Wisconsin possessed a large supply of low-grade ore which required expensive treatment in order to make it merchantable. The statute was designed to assist plant construction by providing a lower tax rate during the construction period. It was also designed to make tax liability in future years correspond to the actual production figures of the plant.

Evidence tended to show that the law had some success. In 1954 a recently formed company, the Ashland Mining Corporation, leased eight hundred acres on the western end of the Penokee range for the purpose of testing the low-grade iron ore potential. The influence of the new tax law was apparent in a contemporary newspaper account:

It will be the first such exploration since a state law was enacted last May to provide tax concessions for mining companies to start operations of that type. An Ashland committee led the campaign for this legislation, similar to that which has long been in effect in Minnesota, a state which has been experiencing a boom in a similar mining endeavor.[18]

The impact of taxes upon the mining industry of Wisconsin through the years was rather conventional. For many years the state struggled rather unsuccessfully with problems of mine valuation. Until these were solved the ad valorem tax was impossible to administer with any degree of correctness. To the legislatures of the nineteenth century, it hardly seemed worthwhile to hire geologists to ascertain mine values scientifically. The Geological Survey was the state agency charged with the duty of finding facts about the state's mineral wealth. But the survey was too busy with other objectives in the nineteenth century to assist with the task of valuation.

The twentieth century witnessed solution of many of the tax problems inherent in application of the ad valorem tax. Generally the solution was to value minerals after they were mined when their quality and quantity were subject to accurate measurements. The twentieth century also brought more use of taxation as a device to encourage and assist an area of the economy characterized by a rather limited base of natural resources. A prime motivating factor, never openly avowed because to do so belittled the state's wealth, was the inability of Wisconsin mineral wealth to stand heavy tax levies. In fact, one might say that throughout the years taxes favored the industry, usually through valuations which probably never exceeded actual value, and in many instances certainly were well below actual value.

In a sense the industry was actually treated favorably by the taxing scheme in force during the nineteenth century. Rather unconsciously the legislatures applied to mining properties a taxing scheme that was so difficult to administer that often assessors assigned very low mineral values to many acres of land. The net effect was a boost to the industry.

8

Government and Industry: A Partnership

AT LEAST FROM the time of Jefferson and Hamilton, debates waxed hot over the relationship of government and private economic enterprise, the proper scope of governmental regulation of business, and the extent and propriety of direct and indirect governmental assistance. Men have affirmed and denied strongly that government should have major credit for the growth of the economy:

[T]hough the Americans conceive themselves to be devoted to *laissez faire* in theory, and to be in practice the most self-reliant of peoples, they have grown no less accustomed than the English to carry the action of the State into ever widening fields.[1]

The present industrial prosperity and all else that exalts and ennobles humanity under the state and federal Constitution are due generally to individual effort and honorable reward without much extraneous aid from governmental meddling in the legitimate business of individuals.[2]

Which appraisal reflects most accurately the course of history? An answer to that question requires marshalling all the available factual data for the many different fields of economic activity. A single segment of the economy of Wisconsin, the mining industry, is our special concern in this paper. In other chapters we have noted roles of both government aid and regulation in developing Wisconsin's mineral resources. Let us here consider certain other respects in which governmental action influenced the framework within which mineral development proceeded.

Support for the first two or three geological surveys came from mineral proprietors who desired to know if lead riches lay beneath the rock strata in areas where early mining efforts converged. After survey geologists had either rendered unfavorable reports, or had dodged the issue, the mineral proprietors sought other means to explore sub-surface conditions at public expense. In 1856 the Linden Mining Company memorialized the state legislature for an appropriation to sink a test shaft into the lower magnesian formation. This memorial provoked majority and minority reports from a special committee composed of lawmakers from the four lead-district counties—Grant, Lafayette, Iowa, and Dane. The majority proposed a bill appropriating $30,000 for the shaft. The minority urged several points in opposition: the precarious state financial picture, the lack of any recommendation from the state geologist, the fact that such an appropriation would give other economic enterprise cause to demand similar aid, the policy of the state constitution against works of internal improvement, and the wisdom of giving "free scope to individual enterprise." [3]

This bill was killed. It was the first of a long series of proposals, memorials, petitions, bills, and reports, all of which sought the same end and all of which suffered the same fate. In 1858 a legislative committee divided on the issue. The 1858 majority recommended against the requested appropriation because times were "hard" and tax collections slow; the minority thought it was "clearly the duty of government" to appropriate money for endeavors beneficial to citizens of the state. In an obvious criticism of the Geological Survey, the disappointed proponents of the 1858 bill observed sarcastically that if the state could spend thousands of dollars for gathering data relevant only to scientific theory, it could well afford a small expenditure to gain practical knowledge desired by mining proprietors. [4]

Feelings in the lead district ran high over the test-shaft proposal. Following one defeat, a Lafayette County representative introduced a resolution of protest. The preamble stated that lead-district taxpayers had paid over thirty thousand tax dollars during the past year; that the requested lead shaft appropriation was but $10,000;

that all building by the state seemed destined for eastern lake-front locations. Accordingly, the proposed resolution declared that the lead district "be and the same is hereby ceded to the United States, for the purpose of forming a new state, to be called PEWABIC, which, in the Chippewa language, means metal, or mineral." [5] The resolution was not enacted. From time to time many influential Wisconsin leaders—Henry Dodge, C. C. Washburn, and others— supported the test-shaft proposal. But proponents of the shaft never came closer to success than winning an occasional approving committee report. As a contemporary newspaper summary put the matter, all the bills went "into the soup." [6]

It is significant that arguments over the test-shaft proposal seldom reached the level of debating the proper role of government in promoting economic development. Usually the opponents argued either that the state was short of funds or that to grant the request would open the door to hundreds of similar requests with no logical stopping place. In a contemporary context, both points were made as arguments of expediency. There was little sign that the debaters felt that a matter of fundamental political or constitutional values was at stake.

Typical nineteenth-century hurry and optimism characterized the handling of the test shaft issue and contributed to the lack of discussion of two relevant points which most certainly bore upon the proposal's wisdom and legality. Only once, at an early stage, did anyone suggest the importance of consulting geologists for their opinion about whether a single shaft would prove much about the total richness of an area covering several counties. Almost all persons at this time took for granted that if lower rock formations were rich in lead at one point, the same would hold true for the entire region. This sanguine opinion and a general hostility to, or skepticism about, scientists in general, and the State Geological Survey in particular, explain the lack of any contact with experts.

The other matter which was almost totally missing from the discussion through the years was whether such an appropriation could be squared with the constitutional command that the state should not "contract any debt for works of internal improvements, or be a party in carrying on such works." Similarly, there was no significant attention to whether the test-shaft project would be included in the implied constitutional prohibition that public funds not be spent for private purposes. That, in years so close to the framing of Wisconsin's constitution, men did not concern themselves with these considerations may suggest that contemporary policy did not oppose state investments designed to promote overall economic growth. If this inference attributes more political philosophy to the times than is warranted, at least the want of debate on such constitutional points shows that contemporary opinion tended toward a narrowly pragmatic appraisal of the questions of subvention or no subvention.

With the exception of agriculture, the mining industry ranked second to no other segment of the economy in ability to secure state funds to search out and disseminate knowledge especially useful to business men. The nature of mining—with all its attendant uncertainties—impelled men to seek for facts to reduce the risks of the hunt for minerals. To a great extent the pressure for both a "practical" geological survey and for a test shaft manifested the miners' thirst for practical knowledge as an asset of their business. The pressure increased when mining activity deserted the surface and went underground. Their inability to secure public funds for a test shaft, and the failure of the state survey to satisfy the narrowly pragmatic demands of the industry, intensified efforts to secure a state mining school. The establishment of a University of Wisconsin Department of Mining and Metallurgy (1871) was not enough to lessen the miners' pressure for a separate school devoted entirely to the mineral industry.

There were unsuccessful attempts in 1889 and in 1893 to set up a school of mines. Finally, in 1907 legislation established the Wisconsin Mining Trade School. Several provisions in the law showed the intention to benefit the lead district. The legislature located the school at Platteville and provided that the governor should appoint to the governing board only persons from the "southwestern part of the state . . . known as the lead district." The course of prescribed study was two years, embracing "geology, mineralogy, chemistry, assaying, mining and mineral surveying and such other branches of practical and theoretical knowledge as will, . . . conduce to the enabling of students . . . to obtain a knowledge of the science, art and practice of mining and the application of machinery thereto." [7]

Financial support for the school came mostly from state appropriations, which gradually increased through the years. Starting with a total state appropriation of $30,000 for the 1907–8 biennium, the amount grew to $83,600 for the year 1950. For a few years, between 1909 and 1915, the legislature sought to encourage cities and counties to appropriate money for support of the school, by providing that the state would reimburse up to two-thirds of a city or county gift. Several acts provided free tuition for certain classes of students (e.g., Wisconsin residents for one year), loans to enable unemployed persons to attend the school during the depression years of the 1930's, and monthly payments to students who were World War I veterans.

For a short time the school gave promise of growing into an important aid to the industry, but the event did not measure up to the promise. In 1917 the course of instruction became three years, and in 1939, four. In 1915 the word "Trade" disappeared from the school's name. In 1939 the school was named the Wisconsin Institute of Technology. More important, the legislature directed that the course of study should "embrace such branches of practical and theoretical knowledge as will . . . give students a knowledge of science, art and practice of engineering." [8] By 1939, then, emphasis had shifted from mining to engineering in general.

Legislation in 1955 abolished the institute's separate governing board, vested control of the school in a thirteen-man Board of Regents of State Colleges, and empowered the board to "maintain a separate state college at Platteville to be known as the Institute of Technology . . . [and a course of instruction which] will . . . give students knowledge of the science, art and practice of general engineering with special emphasis upon mining and civil engineering." [9]

Compared with the mining school, remaining areas of state assistance were minor in impact on the industry. State appropriations financed the purchase of several private mineral collections. Several national and international fairs featured Wisconsin mineral exhibits, notably the Paris Universal Exposition (1867), the Philadelphia Exposition celebrating the centennial of the Declaration of Independence (1876), the Chicago celebration commemorating the four-hundredth anniversary of Columbus' discovery of the New World (1893), and the St. Louis fair shortly after the turn of the century. State pride and a desire to attract people and money to the state motivated participation in these events.

Government fact-finding came into full scope in the twentieth century. Large-scale fact-finding offered a more assured base for lawmaking and also supplied an important aid to industry in making calculations.

Prior to 1890, when Wisconsin sought federal aid for works of internal improvement (such as roads and river projects), lead-production figures backed the requests. But the recorded figures fluctuated widely from document to document because no accurate totals were available. In 1851 the legislature enacted the first statute designed to collect accurate mineral-production figures. From then until 1913 the state's statute books contained provisions dealing with this activity.

The original act required that smelters maintain for public inspection a book showing the amount of ore purchased, the date purchased, the hauler, the owner of the ground, and the owner of the ore. These provisions suggest that a partial purpose of the statute was to facilitate detection of mineral trespassers.

In 1857, after prodding from the state's chief executives, the legislature enjoined city and town assessors to file with the county clerks an annual report of the amount of lead and pig iron produced. The secretary of state was then to tabulate the county returns and inform the legislature of the final totals. The first year's result was disappointing because some counties did not file any report; lead-production figures could scarcely be complete or trustworthy when so important a producing area as Grant County submitted no return.

To secure more complete and accurate returns, an 1858 amendment ordered that county boards of supervisors audit the returns from the local assessors. Results in 1859 and 1860 still displeased Governor Randall, who attributed the unsatisfactory administration to the inexcusable neglect of public officials.

In 1861 the legislature directed that a $25 fine be levied against any assessor who failed to perform his duties. In addition, a delinquent assessor might not have his accounts audited "for any portion of the services rendered by him."

In 1862 the legislature repealed the provision for annual reports and stipulated for collection of data only every tenth year. This change prompted criticism from the governors in 1863, 1866, 1878, and 1881. The usual criticism was that the figures were incomplete, inaccurate, and too costly to procure. In addition, it was repeatedly argued that the time interval was too long for the reports to serve as a basis of policy suggestions. But the legislature did no more experimenting with data collection.

In retrospect, we can see that it was an unfortunate blending of functions, to assign to local tax assessors the duty of quizzing taxpayers about the amount of ore on hand, the amount of ore sold, and the amount of ore raised from a piece of land during a given period. Public officials whose duty was to place property on tax rolls stood little chance of obtaining candid reports on these facts from taxpaying miners.

A large area of governmental assistance to the mining industry consisted of aid in developing transportation facilities, principally to move lead to market. However, we need not review the entire history of road building, canal digging, and railroad construction; the mining industry shared use of these facilities with many other branches of the economy.

Particularly during territorial days and during the first few decades of statehood, the mineral industry demanded more adequate means of transportation. Early lead miners faced tremendous transportation difficulties. Their product was bulky and the market was generally many miles to the east. As noted in Chaper 1, the early miners employed two great water routes—the Mississippi, the Gulf, and the

Atlantic on one hand; the Wisconsin, the Fox, and the Great Lakes on the other. By 1836 miners commenced using overland transportation to Lake Michigan, and by 1847 this route was heavily employed. The Great Lakes route was shorter and preferred because of the speed in remitting sale proceeds. Smelters often operated with little cash and they desperately needed a route which offered quick conversion of minerals into cash. Furthermore, shipping by way of the Missisippi was almost twice as expensive.

Of all Wisconsin minerals, lead demanded more governmental aid for transport than any other mineral. This was true for several reasons. Lead was concentrated in a single geographical area and reached its peak development before other branches of the economy. Hence, lead proprietors were unable to count upon support of other economic blocs for transport demands. The strong political power which the lead area possessed in the early history of Wisconsin contributed to the magnitude and intensity of demands by the lead industry for a better transportation system.

Peak lead production antedated the rail era; consequently most activity centered around the improvement of water routes. In 1838 the lead miner's champion, Colonel Henry Dodge, blueprinted the lead diggers' needs. First, he urged improvement of the mile and a quarter portage between the Fox and Wisconsin rivers; next, he argued for improvement of Mississippi River navigation, particularly the removal of certain rapids near Potosi which in the summer slack-water period grounded lead barges; last, he pleaded for a $2,000 federal appropriation to survey a rail route from Milwaukee to the Mississippi.[10]

Territorial lawmakers attacked the problem of the Mississippi rapids first. The territory itself could not assist because it lacked money. Accordingly, an appeal to Washington for a grant of land followed, and Congress responded on June 15, 1844, by ceding a section of land to the territory, ordering it sold (squatters might buy their land at a figure established by appraisers), and directing that the proceeds be used to "improve Grant River" and for "no other purpose."[11]

Lead miners planned to bypass the Mississippi rapids by channeling navigation around them by way of Grant Creek, which roughly paralleled the Mississippi at the point of difficulty. In 1845 legislation by the territory detailed the machinery for conducting a sale of the federal-aid land, and in 1846 legislation established a commissioner to oversee the actual construction of the bypass. A net profit of $2,725.43 resulted from the sale.

When this amount proved insufficient, both the territorial governor and legislature appealed to Washington for sums slightly in excess of $20,000 to complete the project. In the meantime, the territory attempted to keep the work going by granting power to the town of Potosi to incur a bonded indebtedness of $5,000 to provide funds for the project. When no more federal aid appeared, work stopped and after 1852 no more was done. Memorials to Washington in 1852, 1854, and 1858 asked for sums ranging from $17,000 to $30,000, but these pleas fell upon unsympathetic federal ears and the Potosi episode ended.

When it appeared that the rapids could not be removed, a second plan was drawn up. Lead miners agitated to establish a new town on the Mississippi, downstream from the Potosi rapids. In addition to solving the transportation problem, this new town would enable the lead miners to attain another long cherished objective. As far back as the 1820's, the town of Galena, Illinois, had served as the central market for the lead region. Favorably situated on the Fever River, it was a market for the purchase of lead and a supply point for the food, clothing, tools, and other materials purchased by miners in order to live and to mine ore. Galena merchants prospered, particularly after they commenced the practice of refusing to accept at par bank notes issued by the Bank of Mineral Point.

Lead-area residents founded the new town, Sinipee, but their plan aborted. The locale chosen proved to be so low and swampy, and thus unhealthy, that few persons could be induced to occupy the location. By 1850 decline in lead production and more extensive use of the Great Lakes route doomed both the new town and the Galena monopoly.

Prior to the construction of rail facilities, two other water-improvement projects commanded the attention of lead miners: the improvement of the Rock River and the improvement of the Fox-Wisconsin route. Improvement of the latter would not only aid the movement of lead pigs to eastern manufacturers, but would also transport eastward shot manufactured at the Helena shot tower located high on a bluff overlooking the Wisconsin River west of Madison. Efforts along these two fronts—like those for the Potosi project—quickly took the form of a request to Congress for land grants.

In 1838 Congress granted land to finance work on the Rock River. Lead miners hoped also for funds which would improve navigation on some of the Rock's tributaries, particularly the Pecatonica River, which pierced the heart of the lead region. The lower house of the territorial legislature asked Congress for $20,000 for improvement of the Pecatonica, but Congress did not grant the request. By 1841 a territorial House committee on internal improvements reported a "drying up" of federal funds and urged the legislature to consider granting power to individuals to make the needed improvements.

Nothing of any great value to the lead district resulted from the Rock or Pecatonica plans. Prior to 1850, the lead trade served to buttress most of the arguments for better transportation routes. The Wisconsin government assisted in two ways. First, it served to transmit requests for aid to the federal government. Second, it endowed private, and sometimes public, individuals or groups with authority to undertake improvement work. The precarious condition of territorial and state finances and the state constitutional ban which limited the state from "contracting any debt for works of internal improvement" made impossible any direct territorial or state aid.

Lead moving to eastern markets over the Great Lakes system employed the Erie Canal. Naturally, the toll charges on this part of the move affected the Wisconsin lead smelters directly, and indirectly affected the miners. In 1841 the territorial assembly requested Governor Doty to negotiate with the Governor of New York to abolish or reduce the Erie charges for Wisconsin lead. Moses Strong drafted the appeal and the tolls were reduced. The reduction further enhanced the position of the Great Lakes route over the Mississippi route and made arguments for the Fox-Wisconsin improvement more forceful.

In the eastern markets, Wisconsin lead met competition from Europe. Lead from Europe crossed the Atlantic as ballast; thus the long carrying distance was not a competitive disadvantage for the European product. The issue of tariffs thus presented itself for Wisconsin lead miners' consideration. Quickly the lead miners made up their minds. The miners—usually Jacksonian Democrats and thus hostile to arguments destined to protect eastern manufacturing interests—quickly adopted in entirety the protectionist arguments of Alexander Hamilton.

From 1824 to 1833 Wisconsin lead producers rode the crest of a wave of protectionism. The tariff of 1828, the "Tariff of Abominations," substantially increased the rate on lead. In 1832 an additional duty was placed on scrap lead. In far-off Washington the argument became fierce, and nullification winds threatened to shake down the house of the union. The compromise act (1833) ordered all tariffs gradually reduced so that by June 30, 1842, all duties would be 20 per cent of the value of the goods imported.

The lead district received the 1833 tariff act unfavorably. A territorial House memorial in 1833 spoke the miners' thoughts. The memorial requested reconsideration of the lead tariff issue, presenting all of the protectionists' contentions, as well as pointing out that in 1833 when the act was passed, Wisconsin was not yet a territory and hence was without a spokesman to voice its position. Furthermore, the memorial emphasized that lead was a war metal, hence vital to defense of the nation and entitled to preferential treatment. In 1841 Governor Doty told the legislature that lead from Wisconsin went chiefly through Boston and he hoped that the "intelligent and enterprising merchants of that city . . . [would] receive from this branch of our trade their reward to which they are so justly entitled." [12] When the governor failed to state specifically his own position on the tariff question or to ask for specific legislative action,

he incurred the wrath of the Wisconsin legislature which was still
dominated by the lead region. Murmurings were heard that the Wisconsin Governor was more interested in the prosperity of the merchants of Boston than he was of lead region proprietors. On February 17, 1842, a memorial by the Wisconsin Legislature recited the
past history of federal tariffs on lead and urged more adequate lead
imposts.

The 1842 federal tariff pleased the lead region, and from 1842 to
1848 (the golden age of the lead era) miners prospered under considerable protection. After 1850 the decline in lead production and
the waning of lead influence in the halls at Madison explain the
slackening off of public records showing an interest in the subject
of tariff rates on lead.

Wisconsin public documents from 1850 to the time of World
War II were silent on the tariff question as affecting iron as well as
lead. Most iron-ore competition arose from producers within the
United States and was thus beyond the tariff power of Congress.
After World War II the zinc industry of Wisconsin suffered from
foreign imports, and requests for either a higher tariff or a government stock-piling program were suggested remedies.

The final government aid to the mining industry which should
be noted before concluding this brief survey is the 1959 act granting
water rights to certain mineral proprietors.[13] This law authorized
persons engaged in, or preparing to engage in, mining or processing
ore to apply to the Wisconsin Public Service Commission for permission to divert the water from any lake or stream bordering their
property, to divert such water into another watershed, and to con-
sume the water in the mining or processing operation. The summary
of legislative intent contained in the act demonstrated that its purpose was to encourage and indirectly assist the building of iron-ore
processing plants.

The commission was directed to grant the permit if convinced
that the public benefit from the mining or processing operation out-
weighed the public rights in the stream which the diversion would
eliminate or impair. The act visioned that downstream property

owners bordering on the stream might be injured by the diversion of water, and the law provided that the diverter could acquire the rights of the downstream owners by purchase or condemnation.

Technical experimentation, data collection, professional and technical education, promotion of transport, tariff protection—such is the roster of public aids to the mining industry in Wisconsin. However, positive aid or subsidy is not the only type of legal intervention in economic affairs. The content and scope of legal regulation can also profoundly affect the costs and profits and the direction of growth of productive enterprise. But this aspect of the state's relation to the industry had a limited history. There was little exercise of the police power which bore directly upon the affairs of the miners.

One might imagine that the dangers inherent in mining activities would produce many laws regulating many phases of mine operation. Such was not the case, at least not during the nineteenth century. The industry was given an almost free rein to operate as it pleased. What few nineteenth-century regulations existed made only minor impact. Many incorporated cities were granted power to prohibit the sinking of shafts in city streets. In 1876 a State Board of Health was created, but for many years it limited its operations to requiring mining company physicians to coöperate in collecting information. An 1893 statute prohibited polluting streams with "saw dust, lime, or other deleterious substance." An earlier law (1848) sought to assure accuracy in scales weighing ore. This short list demonstrates the minor role nineteenth-century regulatory laws played in the history of Wisconsin minerals.

The twentieth century saw more regulation, much of it already covered in earlier chapters. In addition to regulations already discussed, the most important were laws which attempted to insure safe construction of mine shafts. In 1947 the Industrial Commission was authorized to issue permits to construct mine shafts, provided the commission was satisfied that certain standards of safety were met. In 1953 a more elaborate statute regulated the abandonment of mine shafts.

9

Economic Goals and Legal Functions

TO ASSESS THE legal history of an industry is to bring events under two judgments—that of their relation to certain economic goals, and that of their relation to values and trends which respond to political rather than to market processes.

We may naturally, therefore, sum up the relations between the mining industry and the law in Wisconsin under two principal heads. First are the relations between the law and the industry, considered as a system of economic action. Under this head we need review the law's performance affecting fulfillment of the industry's needs for land, money capital, entrepreneurial skills, and labor. Second, because the law itself constitutes a system of action, we need review the demands which the growth of the mining industry made upon legal process, and the distinctive roles of legislative, judicial, and executive or administrative authority in response.

Law and the Factors of Production

That law legitimated private ownership of the bulk of mineral wealth in Wisconsin was an important factor in developing private mining industry. Entrepreneurs and miners alike were vitally concerned about the legal terms of access to mineral-bearing lands. During about the first half of the nineteenth century, the United States retained ownership of the mineral lands in the state, but sanctioned private mining industry within the framework of government leases. However, this program encountered great hostility from the miners, and even those who took leases were dissatisfied with such tenure. Near mid-century these pressures from the industry—given the more impetus, because they accorded with the general impatience for immediate economic growth—induced Congress to abandon its insistence on leasing. So Congress allowed disposition of the fee simple title to mineral-bearing public lands. Thus it passed the full initiative of decision over mineral resources to private decision makers. Federal action in this way foreclosed the state from free opportunity to determine its own basic title policy toward this type of resource. The bulk of the mineral-bearing lands in Wisconsin passed directly from the federal government to private owners, by way of public and private sales, pre-emption, and grants of homesteads, of bounties, and of gifts in aid of works of internal improvement. Never in the nineteenth century was the state in a legal or practical position to elect whether it might retain in state ownership the control of access to all or part of the mineral wealth within its boundaries.

That federal action narrowed the possible range of state choice is worth noting, to help assess responsibility for the course of policy. On the other hand, to observe that the state's range of choice was narrowed is not to imply that the state would likely have chosen differently than the Congress in dealing with the mineral lands. The federal leasing program developed sharp local antagonism toward the idea that government might be a perpetual or longtime landlord. Wisconsin was a frontier economy; men's experience there taught them faith that general welfare was served by promoting individual striving and creativity. No strong interest bloc existed to argue for retaining in public hands the ultimate title to non-renewable natural resources; on the contrary, the constantly felt pressure of scarcity of private working capital urged men to find immediate solutions in making readily and cheaply available the natural wealth of the public domain. The bias of contemporary opinion was not to favor an abstract individualism. Where men could see practical point for advancing productivity, in a strong use of public power, they did not hesitate to use it. Thus, despite the general favor for private fee simple ownership as the norm of land tenure, Wisconsin's legislature granted the right of eminent domain to mineral land proprietors, who sought to develop their holdings by conducting water across the lands of neighbors who would not voluntarily give them such access. Speedy, maximum increase of productivity was the over-riding value. Generally, however, prevailing opinion believed that this value was best achievevd by broad dispersion of economic decision-making into private hands. In this perspective we can well believe that the state would have made no more sustained effort than did the United States, to establish itself as longtime landlord of its mineral wealth.

By inattention, rather than by any demonstrated deliberate choice, the state long coupled with this favor for private fee simple ownership of the mineral lands a failure to make any substantial use of its police power to express public interest in the manner in which men used their titles. The law left to the unchecked discretion of private decision-makers the manner of minerals exploitation. Law accepted and enforced private mineral-lands leases on the terms which the parties set for developing these resources. Types of mining practices, and the speed and timing of mining activity, were determined solely by the focus and urgency of private interest. This pattern of affairs undoubtedly speeded up and increased the volume of mining activity. On the other hand, it took no account of social values or costs other than those which inhered in such private operations. Moreover, in the contemporary emphasis upon opportunistic speed there is indication that the community lost some of the advantages of variety and experiment which energetic private dealing might be supposed to promote; at least in their legal arrangements, these impatient operators early fell into set patterns of dealing, and, for example, made word-for-word copies of each other's corporate charters.

That nineteenth-century Wisconsin looked upon law as an instrument to be used freely and positively to advance production was clear in the resort to legal devices to help solve the chronic scarcity of money capital. In common with its times, early Wisconsin politics showed hostility to the corporate device. This antagonism was at first given point by some early ill-fated ventures in Wisconsin, notably by the misfortunes of the Bank of Mineral Point. But incorporation offered too useful a means to muster capital for business ventures, to be left long unused. Not only did men seek corporate charters in increasing number, but the legislature showed generous response to their demands. Legislation lifted restrictions early set upon corporate powers; early restrictions on the extent of corporate land holdings, upon maximum capital, and upon corporate life, were liberalized and tended to disappear. By its readiness to act upon applications for special corporate charters, the legislature emphasized public approval of corporate organization in specific instances, and in effect invited promoters to shape the content of charters to their own specifications. We must not exaggerate the extent of specially tailored corporate organization thus created; the bustle of these opportunistic times made men impatient with spending time on much formal planning or calculation, and draftsmen of special corporate charters tended on the whole to make liberal borrowing of charter terms which they found already on the books. Even so, the volume of special charters in this relatively simple economy attested the importance which promoters attached to the corporate form as an aid in mustering capital, and there were enough special provisions to bear witness to men's conscious efforts to use law to overcome the scarcity of cash capital. Special tax provisions helped conserve working capital. Special exemptions from the general legal regulations of usurious interest helped venturesome enterprises bid for capital.

Mining promoters also saw the state geological survey as a means to help them win investors' money from competing uses. In their confident view the survey would report favorably upon mining prospects, and these reports would induce capital to join the industry. So, too, the industry pressed for state provision of minerals exhibits at fairs and expositions which might publicize Wisconsin investment opportunities. There was striking testimony that legal action could take on its own institutional force, in the resistance which the geological survey management showed to the manipulative ambitions of the mining speculators. There is little evidence that the law's direct promotional efforts bore fruit for the industry, apart from the undoubted help which the ready availability of incorporation afforded in mustering investment. On the other hand, the want of adequate legal regulation of investment practices allowed free scope to ill-advised or dishonest enticement of a good deal of investment capital. In this aspect the condition of contemporary legal order worked to facilitate the flow of money into mining enterprise, but not in a manner which could be counted a constructive contribution to the economy or to general social values.

The provision of an industry's investment and working capital is affected also by the extent to which law enforces upon the industry proper contributions to the general costs of social order. Through the nineteenth century, Wisconsin's tax system was ill-adjusted to the special problems of identifying and valuing subsurface mineral wealth. In this aspect, the law's defects again worked to ease the financing problems of the industry; had administration of the general property tax worked with efficiency, it would have fastened the normal burden of that tax upon mineral wealth with such harshness as to have generated strong industry pressure for taxation specially adapted to the peculiar problems of mining enterprise. The industry showed little concern with the formal pattern of tax law through most of its history. The fact was mute witness to the contribution which loose administration of the formal law made to easing the industry's financial difficulties. Again, we must note the fact, but can hardly count it a type of constructive contribution of law to economic development.

The prime problem which mining-industry labor brought to law through the period of this study concerned employers' liability for injuries suffered by workers on the job. Before the workmen's compensation act of 1911, the injured employee had a hard road to obtaining damages in law. The employer was, in general, liable only if he were deemed at fault in a respect which contributed to cause the injury, and legal fault was often a hard issue to establish. If the injured employee surmounted the difficulty of proving fault, his recovery might yet be barred by any of the quite readily established defenses of contributory negligence, assumption of risk, or injury caused by the negligence of a fellow servant. The deeper grounds of policy were not clearly stated in this total pattern of doctrine. However, the effect was to reduce the financial risks and burdens of mining enterprise to the entrepreneur, and largely to cast the incidence of loss from personal injury in the first instance upon the worker and his dependents, and at second remove upon the general taxpayer and public charity. So viewed, the law's relation to the problem of personal injury adds another item to what was obviously a major type of influence upon the course of the industry—the reduction of direct money demands upon private enterprise, by the omissions and defects of legally declared values and legal administration.

In most respects, we should remember, the development of the mining industry did not have unique connections with legal order. Mining was not the only economic enterprise which either sought or in practical effect obtained support from legal institutions. Law provided the general framework of contract and property for market dealing, furnished means of organizing finance, credit, and management through banking and business corporations, and offered the protection of the criminal law and the law of tort to the orderly pursuit of private planning and private decision-making. Public subsidies helped create means of bulk transport by road, by water, and by rail, and thus provided assistance indispensable to the growth of all production which, like that in the mining industry, depended upon facilities for moving to market heavy, bulky, low-unit-price commodities. That the mining business shared such general benefits of legal order with other kinds of enterprise carries the important reminder that the most fundamental contribution which law made to the course of the industry was in helping sustain the total organization of the society and the economy in which the industry took a part.

Roles of the Principal Legal Agencies

The roles of the major legal agencies overlap, both in definition and adoption of values, and in application of formally declared values in concrete instances. However, the overlap does not negate the functional reality of the existence of different agency roles. When we consider law as a system of action viewed in the context of United States history, the separation of powers emerges as more than a doctrinal concept; in terms of the distinctive jobs done by different agencies, appraisal of the separation of powers uncovers dimensions of legal experience otherwise lost to our accounting.

For the mining industry during the period covered by this survey, especially in the nineteenth century, the legislature was by far the most important agency of legal order. This estimate is reinforced, if we count as part of the legislative process—as is proper—the program-shaping role of the chief executive. For better or worse, the legislature was the principal organ by which public policy bearing specifically on the mining industry was declared. Policy was made through the legislative process with little check or hindrance and with little guidance from either executive or judicial agencies. Statute law set the terms of access to mineral-bearing land, defined policy toward trespass against mineral wealth, provided the framework of incorporation for business ventures, and determined the lawful rates of interest and the terms of taxation which affected the conditions of industry finance. The governors, in their role as assessors of state-wide public interest, helped articulate issues and urge them to legislative decision. Almost always, however, the governor left particular decision of policy to the legislative process; generally the chief executive did not even voice preference for any specific course of action or argue the merits of competing choices, and rarely did he employ the veto.

The quality of operation of the legislative process was poor. The defects concerned more basic matters than craftsmanship in the particular execution of the legislative jobs. There was much clumsy drafting, marked by ambiguity and contradiction, and failure to make regular review of the statues to eliminate obsolete material and achieve better order and consistency. But more fundamental defects in the working of legislative process lay not so much in formal technique as in general approach.

Especially in the first generation after statehood (from 1848 into the seventies), the legislature too often dealt piecemeal with large public issues. Fragmented, episodic attention characterized legislative treatment of problems of realizing mineral wealth. A striking example of the piecemeal approach was in the grant of special corporate charters. In mining-industry situations, the legislature also made piecemeal alterations or adaptations of the state's general policy on usury, on eminent domain, and on taxation. The legislature even put regulations carrying penal sanctions into special mining charters, with no apparent concern for the particular issues this practice raised, of fair notice and equal protection of the laws. Piecemeal legislation drained legislative time, atomized decision-making, and fostered ambiguities in policy in matters in which uniformity was attainable and hence wiser and fairer. Most objectionable, from the standpoint of promoting proper and rational public policy-making, was that fragmented legislation tended to veil issues. When a special corporate charter permitted a particular company to pay a higher interest rate than the general usury law allowed, the import of the provision—if it had such practical effect as the promoters obviously sought—was to provide a special legal benefit, to divert capital from other potential uses to this favored use. In effect such legislation implied a preference in law among competitors for investment capital. But when the matter was formally presented in the narrow context of a particular charter, this approach lost to view the general questions as to what hierarchy of investment options should receive the encouragement of law.

The nineteenth-century Wisconsin legislature was ill-equipped in attitude, experience, or staff to deal with the rush of events in the growth of the state. In the development of the mining industry, as in other fields, events moved so fast that important choices were made through legislation in effect by default rather than by calculation. Thus the impatience of prevailing opinion to spur economic expansion overcame the feeble effort at a federal mineral-lands leasing program. So, also, under the push of events the state legislature made only imperfect definition of the task of the geological survey, leaving ambiguous whether its mission was to serve as a promotional aid to mining entrepreneurs, as an agency of scientific research, or as an instrument of general economic planning. That the geological survey resisted the self-seeking interests which sought to warp its findings, and set a precedent for honest staff work in state policy-making, was due to the character of its own management, and owed little to leadership or protection provided by the legislature.

If legislative process worked poorly because it tended to handle problems piecemeal and with too ready response to the most immediate pressure of events, its failure to provide a strong pattern of policy stemmed also from relative indifference to its fact-finding responsibility. Because the formal act of decision (enacting a statute) is more focused and dramatic, and relieves the tensions created by the necessity of choice, this aspect of legislative process tended unduly to pre-empt men's attention. Basic to reasonable and responsible decision is the definition of alternatives and the determination of facts relevant to defining and evaluating choices. But in shaping law affecting the mining industry, as in other major fields of contemporary policy, nineteenth-century legislators characteristically slighted their function of inquiry, to press impatiently to formal action. Despite the substantial importance of mineral wealth in the early Wisconsin economy, legislative records show no substantial legislative investigation of the course of the industry and its relationships to the over-all development of the state. Even when the legislature delegated its investigative role to the geological survey, it did so carelessly without comprehending the magnitude and difficulties of the task it assigned; hence it demanded more from the survey than was reasonable in light of the money and time allotted for the job, and provided little support to arm the survey against the special interests which pressed on it. It is true that public policy cannot move far ahead of fairly broad currents of knowledge and opinion. It would be unrealistic to criticize mid-nineteenth-century Wisconsin legislators because they did not at one stroke evolve a broad policy on conservation of natural resources or enact a fair and balanced program to guide the incidence of losses from injuries suffered by workers on the job. However, with its power of investigation and its control of the public purse, the legislature stands under responsibility to help advance the acquisition of facts and the consideration of values, so that over time men may mature wiser judgments upon the terms of social life. Until near the end of the nineteenth century the Wisconsin legislature behaved with large indifference to this responsibility; though we should not ask that conservation or industrial-accidents policies be born before their time, clearly the want of provision to collect reliable data on elementary facts of minerals production, income, and costs, or on industrial accidents, meant unwarranted delay in bringing to responsible deliberation and decision matters of broad public concern.

The executive branch of government played, on the whole, a more limited role affecting the mining industry than did the legislature. As potential spokesman for a state-wide constituency, as an officer constitutionally charged to advise the legislature on "the condition of the state," and as a leading party figure, the governor was part of the legislative process. But the office lacked a tradition or expectation of strong policy leadership, and, as we have seen, the governors typically limited themselves to relatively noncommittal note of some mining-industry matters, and to limited and episodic use of the veto. There is little to say of executive action in the distinctive sense of the term, for through most of the period covered by this volume legislation made little call upon public administration to implement public policy. The large reliance upon market processes for ordering economic affairs—reflected in the central roles of the law of private property and contract and the law of private business corporations—meant that public scrutiny upon what was done took place chiefly through the courts, as these decided lawsuits between private parties. The central state executive apparatus was small and unspecialized through most of the mining industry history; aside from the geological survey (which, moreover, was more a delegate of the legislature than an office of state administration), state executive action had little relation to the industry until the creation in the twentieth century of the Industrial Commission and the Tax Commission. Nineteenth-century public administration had most connection with mining development through local government tax authorities, but tax law bore with no specialized impact upon the affairs of the industry.

The courts might have affected the course of the mining industry through any of three channels—applying the federal or state constitutions, interpreting statutes, or declaring and applying common law. In practice the judiciary had substantial connection with the industry's affairs only through the common law. This pattern in itself reflected the limited extent to which the legislative process generated broad policy affecting the industry. Constitutional doctrine figured in a few, limited instances in the legislative process, when a committee report or a governor's veto raised constitutional scruples, usually over a piece of special legislation. But the course of legislative activity was so limited that it simply did not produce occasions for judicial intervention to add to the content of public policy, in the name either of constitutional or statutory interpretation. On the other hand, in passing on the validity, meaning, or application of mining titles and leases and of business arrangements and contracts, and in adjudicating suits arising out of industrial accidents, the judges brought a substantial body of common law to bear upon the industry's affairs. What is most striking about this impress of common law on the industry is its silent testimony to the institutional weight of the law itself. The fact situations peculiar to mining activity of course colored the invocation of general doctrines of property, contract, and tort. But, on the whole, these common law decisions show relatively little declaration of public policy distinctive to mining-industry affairs. On the contrary, they reflect the strong tendency of the judges to bring the problems presented by the industry's activity within the framework of more generalized values and procedures. This outcome is not surprising. Partly it reflects the extent of delegation of social order in this field to the market and to the areas of law which sustain and implement market dealing, for the market exerts pressure towards generalized forms of transactions or relations which facilitate a multiplicity of dealings. Partly it reflects the traditional limitations of judicial process; within the separation of powers, the creation of new and specialized public policy rests with the legislature.

The growth of the Wisconsin mining industry and the operations of Wisconsin legal order had numerous and important relations. Yet, an assessment of the functional roles played by the several major legal agencies leaves the judgment that, on the whole, legal process dealt shallowly with issues of public concern distinctive to the industry. If this judgment is warranted, it points to the central fact of a weak legislative process. For in the legislature resided the basic means, and hence the basic responsibility, to move public policy making into more significant relation to the reach and depth of novel problems of social relationships. This judgment should remind us, too, that no more fundamental task was demanded of legal process in this mobile society than that it help men to make rational and humane adjustment to the social change which insistently pressed upon them. So weighed, the nineteenth-century record of law's dealings with the mining industry pointed up by contrast the extent of the challenge which the growing complexity of affairs put upon the legal order of the twentieth century.

Notes, Index

Notes

CHAPTER I

1 John Wills Taylor, "Reservation and Leasing of the Salines, Lead and Copper Mines of the Public Domain" (Unpublished Ph.D. Thesis, University of Chicago, 1930).

2 Reuben Gold Thwaites, *Notes on Early Lead Mining in the Fever (or Galena) River Region,* Wisconsin Historical Collections, Vol. XIII (Madison, Wis., 1895), p. 271.

3 William Francis Raney, *Wisconsin: A Story of Progress* (New York, 1940), p. 90; Alice E. Smith, *James Duane Doty: A Frontier Promoter* (Madison, Wis., 1954), p. 80.

4 "Early History of Wisconsin," *Mineral Point Tribune* (Wisconsin), December 9, 1875.

5 Louis Albert Copeland, *The Cornish in Southwestern Wisconsin,* Wisconsin Historical Collections, Vol. XIV (Madison, Wis., 1898), p. 301.

6 Joseph Schafer, *The Wisconsin Lead Region* (Madison, Wis., 1932), chap. vii.

7 Glines, "Reminiscences of Early Times in the Lead Mines of Illinois and Wisconsin," Shullsburg *Pick and Gad* (Wisconsin), March 22, 1884.

8 "Report of the Committee on Mining and Smelting," *Journal of the Assembly,* 23 Legis. (1870), p. 485; Glines, "Reminiscences," Shullsburg *Pick and Gad,* March 22, 1884.

9 Ellis Baker Usher, *Wisconsin: Its Story and Biography, 1848–1913* (Chicago, 1914), I, 128, quoting the *Journal of Science and Arts* for July, 1842.

10 Frederick Merk, *Economic History of Wisconsin in the Civil War Decade* (Madison, Wis., 1916), pp. 114–15.

11 *Ibid.,* p. 120.

12 *Appleton Crescent* (Wisconsin), February 18, 1865, p. 3.

13 *Geology of Wisconsin,* Vol. III (Madison, Wis., 1880), p. 357.

14 Ulysses S. Grant, *Preliminary Report on the Copper Bearing Rocks of Douglas County, Wisconsin,* Geological and Natural History Survey Bulletin, No. VI (2d ed., Madison, Wis., 1901), p. 76.

15 James M. Swank, *The American Iron Trade in 1876,* Booklet prepared for the American Iron and Steel Association (Philadelphia, 1876). The figure is set at 14 by another writer: Smith, *James Duane Doty,* p. 16.

16 Orin Grant Libby, *Significance of the Lead and Shot Trade in Early Wisconsin History,* Wisconsin Historical Collections, Vol. XIII (Madison, Wis., 1895), p. 293.

CHAPTER 2

1 *Journals of the American Congress from 1774 to 1788* (Washington: Way and Gideon, 1823), IV, 520–21.

2 The Case of Mines, 1 Plow. 310, 75 English Reprint 472 (King's Bench, 1568).

3 See Charles A. Beard and Mary R. Beard, *Basic History of the United States* (New York, 1944), p. 5; *Shoemaker* v. *United States,* 147 U.S. 282, at p. 306 (1892); Thomas C. Donaldson, *The Public Domain* (Washington, 1844), p. 306.

4 1 U.S. Stats. at L. (1854), c. 29, § 2, 464–66; 2 U.S. Stats. at L. (1854), 73, 78.

5 2 U.S. Stats. at L. (1854), c. 26, § 6, 324–28.

6 2 U.S. Stats. at L. (1854), c. 49, § 5, 448–49.

7 See John Wills Taylor, "Reservation and Leasing of the Salines, Lead and Copper Mines of the Public Domain" (Unpublished Ph.D. Thesis, University of Chicago, 1930); Ann Keppel, "Attempts to Formulate and Administer a Federal Lead Land Policy" (Unpublished M.A. Thesis, University of Wisconsin, 1954).

8 *Annals of Congress,* 17 Cong., 2 Sess. (1822–23), 18.

9 See *American State Papers* (*Public Lands*) (Washington, 1860), V, 589 ff.

10 Another source supplies the following figures:

1821 to 1831

Lead Dug (pounds)	5,151,252
Rent Lead (pounds)	423,329
Expenses	$14,184.26

Source: *American State Papers* (*Public Lands*) (Washington, 1861), VIII, 450.

11   *Annals of Congress,* 13 Cong., 3 Sess. (1814–15), 1131.

12   *Annals of Congress,* 17 Cong., 2 Sess. (1822–23), 237.

13   *Ibid.,* 242.

14   *Congressional Debates,* Vol. III (Washington, 1829), p. 54, col. 2.

15   4 U.S. Stats. at L. (1854), c. 55, 364.

16   4 U.S. Stats. at L. (1854), c. 76, § 4, 686.

17   Keppel, "Lead Land Policy," p. 98. Grant County lands were opened for sale in November, 1834; Iowa and Lafayette County lands on September 7 and 21, respectively.—Merville K. Hobbs, *John and Sarah Bradbury Coons and their Descendants* [Chicago, 1939], p. 29; Alice E. Smith, *James Duane Doty* (Madison, Wis., 1954), p. 129.

18   Joseph Schafer, *The Wisconsin Lead Region* (Madison, Wis., 1932), pp. 83 ff; Taylor, "Reservation and Leasing," pp. 121 ff; Keppel, "Lead Land Policy," pp. 101 ff; House Ex. Doc. 277, 27 Cong., 2 Sess. (1842).

19   The language of this Act is quoted on p. 35.

20   One estimate is that 72,000 acres were still reserved at the time Strong made his move. David D. Van Tassel, "Democracy, Frontier, and Mineral Point" (Unpublished M.A. Thesis, University of Wisconsin, 1951), p. 15.

21   Ops. Atty. Gen. U.S. (Washington, 1837), III, 277.

22   David D. Owen, *Report of a Geological Exploration of Part of Iowa, Wisconsin, and Illinois in 1839,* House Ex. Doc. 239, 26 Cong., 1 Sess.

23   Senate Ex. Doc. 407, 28 Cong., 1 Sess.

24   *Journal of the Council,* 1 Legis., 2 Sess. (Madison, Wis., 1837), pp. 32–33.

25   *United States* v. *Gratiot,* 14 Peters 526 (U.S., 1840).

26   *United States* v. *Gear,* 3 Howard 120 (U.S., 1845).

27   *Cong. Globe,* 28 Cong., 1 Sess., Appendix, 327, col. 2.

28   *Ibid.,* p. 4777.

29   *Cong. Globe,* 29 Cong., 1 Sess., 85.

30   *Ibid.,* pp. 898–99.

31   9 U.S. Stats. at L. (1846), 37.

32   Taylor, "Reservation and Leasing," pp. 229 ff.

33   9 U.S. Stats. at L. (1846), 51.

CHAPTER 3

1   *Journal of the Senate,* 1 Legis. (1848), p. 399.

2   *Journal of the Senate,* 2 Legis. (1849), pp. 92, 97.

3   John Goadby Gregory, *The Land-Limitations Movement: A Wisconsin Episode of 1848-1851,* Parkman Club Papers No. 14 (Milwaukee, Wis., 1897).

4 Wis. Laws (1917), J. Res. 15.
5 Wis. Laws (1923), J. Res. 41.
6 *Wisconsin Bluebook* (Madison, Wis., 1937), p. 108.
7 Ops. Atty. Gen. Wis. (Madison, Wis., 1919), p. 410.
8 Wis. Laws (1903), c. 450, § 16.
9 Wis. Laws (1917), c. 454, § 15.
10 Wis. Laws (1951), c. 279.
11 Wis. Laws (1909), c. 374.
12 Wis. Laws (1911) c. 452.
13 Wis. Laws (1917), c. 282, § 10; c. 454, § 45.
14 Wis. Laws (1925), c. 159.
15 *Journal of the Senate,* 50 Legis. (1911), p. 134, J. Res. 28 S.
16 Orin Grant Libby, *Significance of the Lead and Shot Trade in Early Wisconsin History,* Wisconsin Historical Collections, Vol. XIII (Madison, Wis., 1895), p. 293.
17 Wis. Rev. Stats. (1849), c. 134, § 49.
18 Wis. Rev. Stats. (1865), c. 377, § 4. Commissioners of School and University Lands and Commissioners of Public Lands are the same body.
19 *Ibid.*
20 Wis. Laws (1905), c. 264, § 15.
21 Wis. Gen. Laws (1871), c. 21, § 2.
22 Wis. Laws (1905), c. 264, § 12.
23 Wis. Gen. Laws (1864), c. 193.
24 Wis. Gen. Laws (1865), c. 520.
25 Wis. Laws (1893), c. 60, § 1.
26 Wis. Laws (1895), c. 34.
27 Wis. Laws (1860), c. 277.
28 Wis. Laws (1891), c. 320.
29 See quotation from Libby, *Significance of the Lead and Shot Trade* on page 16, above.
30 See *Phillips* v. *Geesland,* 2 Piney 120 (Wis., 1849); *Knowlton* v. *Culver,* 2 Piney 86 (Wis., 1849); *Gillett* v. *Treganza,* 6 Wis. 343 (1858); *Bracken* v. *Preston,* 1 Piney 584 (Wis., 1845); *Phoenix Lead Mining & Smelting Company* v. *Sydnor,* 39 Wis. 600 (1876).
31 Wis. Terr. Laws (1836), p. 53, Act No. 23.
32 Wis. Terr. Laws (1838), p. 195; see also Wis. Terr. Laws (1848), p. 15.
33 Wis. Gen. Laws (1860), c. 260.
34 *St. Anthony Mining and Milling Company* v. *Shaffra,* 138 Wis. 507, 509, 120 N.W. 238, 239 (1909).
35 See *Raisbeck* v. *Anthony,* 73 Wis. 572, 41 N.W. 72 (1889).
36 Wis. Gen. Laws (1860), c. 260, § 5.

37 *Loveland* v. *Longhenry,* 145 Wis. 60, 129 N.W. 650 (1911).
38 Revisors' Notes contained in Wis. Rev. Stats. (1898), §§ 1650–55.
39 Wis. Laws (1880), c. 283.
40 "First Annual Report of the State Geologist," *Journal of the Senate,* 7 Legis. (1854), Appendix, p. 42, Doc. H.
41 See *Townsend* v. *Peasley,* 35 Wis. 383 (1874).
42 Charter of the Dodgeville Mining and Manufacturing Company, Wis. Priv. Laws (1853), c. 388.

CHAPTER 4

1 Quoted in Ellis Baker Usher, *Wisconsin: Its Story and Biography* (Chicago, 1914), I, 127.
2 Orin Grant Libby, *Significance of the Lead and Shot Trade in Early Wisconsin History,* Wisconsin Historical Collections, Vol. XIII (Madison, Wis., 1895), pp. 293 ff.
3 See "Report of the Committee on Mining and Smelting," *Journal of the Assembly,* 5 Legis. (1852), Appendix, pp. 263 ff.; "Report of the Committee on Mining and Smelting," *Journal of the Senate,* 6 Legis. (1853), Appendix; "First Annual Report of the State Geologist," *Journal of the Senate,* 7 Legis. (1854), Appendix Doc. H; *Journal of the Senate* (1853), pp. 11–18; (1854), pp. 21–22; (1864), p. 15; (1869), p. 22; (1871), Appendix, p. 11.
4 5 U.S. Stats. at L. (1856), c. 331, 61.
5 5 U.S. Stats. at L. (1856), c. 75, 198.
6 Editorial in Madison *Wisconsin Inquirer,* Dec. 12, 1840.
7 Wis. Terr. Laws (1838), Act No. 16.
8 Wis. Const. (1848), Art. XI, § 1.
9 "Report of the Committee on Incorporations," *Journal of the Senate* (1848), p. 219.
10 Wis. Priv. Laws (1853), c. 17, § 6. The provision was repealed one year later.
11 Wis. Priv. Laws (1853), c. 206.
12 Wis. Priv. Laws (1854), c. 95.
13 See *Journal of the Senate,* 23 Legis. (1880), pp. 341, 500.
14 Benjamin P. Thomas, *Abraham Lincoln* (New York, 1952), p. 29.
15 Wis. Priv. Laws (1866), c. 529.
16 78 Wis. 427, 431, 47 N.W. 726, 727 (1891).
17 Henry Colin Campbell, *Wisconsin in Three Centuries* (New York, 1906), Vol. IV, ch. ix.
18 *Ibid.,* p. 235.

19 *Warner* v. *Bates,* 75 Wis. 278, 43 N.W. 957 (1889).
20 *Warner* v. *Benjamin,* 89 Wis. 290, 62 N.W. 179 (1895).
21 *Ibid.*
22 *Journal of the Senate* (1851), p. 711.
23 Wis. Const., Art IV, § 7.
24 Wis. Laws (1913), c. 756, § 1753–50 (4).
25 Wis. Laws (1913), c. 756, § 1753–51 (4) (a) and (b).

CHAPTER 5

1 See Gordon M. Haferbecker, *Wisconsin Labor Laws* (Madison, Wis., 1958); Gertrude Schmidt, "History of Labor Legislation in Wisconsin," (Unpublished Ph.D. Thesis, University of Wisconsin, 1933); Harry Weiss, "The Development of Workmen's Compensation in the United States," (Unpublished Ph.D. Thesis, University of Wisconsin, 1933).
2 *Strahlendorf* v. *Rosenthal,* 30 Wis. 674 (1872).
3 *Jones* v. *Florence Mining Company,* 66 Wis. 268, 28 N.W. 207 (1886).
4 *Paule* v. *Florence Mining Company,* 80 Wis. 350, 50 N.W. 189 (1891).
5 *McMahon* v. *Ida Mining Company,* 95 Wis. 308, 70 N.W. 478 (1897); another opinion in 101 Wis. 102, 76 N.W. 1098 (1898).
6 *Adams* v. *Snow,* 106 Wis. 152, 81 N.W. 983 (1900).
7 *Heathcock* v. *Milwaukee-Platteville Lead and Zinc Mining Company,* 128 Wis. 46, 107 N.W. 463 (1906).
8 *Butteris* v. *Mifflin and Linden Mining Company,* 133 Wis. 343, 113 N.W. 642 (1907).
9 *Winkler* v. *Power and Mining Manufacturing Company,* 141 Wis. 244, 124 N.W. 273 (1910); *Jakopac* v. *Newport Mining Company,* 152 Wis. 177, 139 N.W. 820 (1913); *Dolphin* v. *Peacock Mining Company,* 155 Wis. 439, 144 N.W. 1112 (1914); *Mayhew* v. *Wisconsin Zinc Company,* 158 Wis. 112, 147 N.W. 1035 (1914).
10 Wis. Laws (1911), c. 50.
11 Wis. Laws (1913), c. 519.
12 See Wis. Laws (1911), c. 485, § 1021 b-2.
13 Amendments in the law after 1911 left the law basically unchanged. Some amendments were necessary from time to time to keep pace with increased costs and to remedy oversights. For example, the allotment for reasonable burial expenses originally set at $100 increased to $200 in 1923, to $300 in 1945, and then to $350 in 1953. The original law covered payments for medical and surgical expenses, but failed to cover the injured employee's hospital bills. These were added in 1913.

14 See Haferbecker, *Wisconsin Labor Laws,* p. 42.

15 *Ibid.,* pp. 62–63.

16 Wis. Laws (1919), c. 457. Wis. Laws (1919), c. 668, further clarified the intent by extending the act to ". . . all other injuries, including occupational diseases, growing out of and incidental to the employment."

17 *Wisconsin Granite Company* v. *Industrial Commission,* 208 Wis. 270, 273–74, 242 N.W. 191, 192 (1932).

18 *Schaefer* v. *Industrial Commission,* 185 Wis. 317, 201 N.W. 396 (1924).

19 *Employers Mutual Life Insurance Company* v. *McCormick,* 195 Wis. 410, 217 N.W. 738 (1928).

20 *Montello Granite Company* v. *Industrial Commission,* 197 Wis. 428, 222 N.W. 315 (1928).

21 *Falk Corporation* v. *Industrial Commission,* 202 Wis. 284, 232 N.W. 542 (1930).

22 *Zurich General Accident and Life Insurance Company* v. *Industrial Commission,* 203 Wis. 135, 146–47, 233 N.W. 772 (1930).

23 See *Kimlark Rug Corp.* v. *Industrial Commission,* 210 Wis. 319, 246 N.W. 424 (1933).

24 *Wisconsin Granite Company* v. *Industrial Commission,* 208 Wis. 270, 242 N.W. 191 (1932).

25 *Kanneberg* v. *Industrial Commission,* 212 Wis. 651, 250 N.W. 821 (1933).

26 *Montreal Mining Company* v. *Industrial Commission,* 225 Wis. 1, 272 N.W. 828 (1937).

27 See *North End Foundry Co.* v. *Industrial Commission,* 217 Wis. 363, 258 N.W. 439 (1935), where employee was discharged before any wage loss and employer was held not liable.

28 Wis. Laws (1935), c. 465.

29 See case cited in note 27, supra where employees were discharged after medical examinations demanded by the insurance carrier showed silicotic conditions.

30 Wis. Laws (1935), c. 465.

31 See *North End Foundry Co.* v. *Industrial Commission,* supra note 27, at p. 373; *Schaefer & Co.* v. *Industrial Commission,* 220 Wis. 289, 265 N.W. 390 (1936), at p. 295.

32 *Milwaukee M. & G. I. Works* v. *Industrial Commission,* 220 Wis. 244, 263 N.W. 662 (1936); *Schaefer & Co.* v. *Industrial Commission,* supra note 31.

33 *North End Foundry Co.* v. *Industrial Commission,* supra note 27, at p. 373.

34 Wis. Laws (1935), c. 465.
35 Wis. Laws (1937), c. 180.
36 Wis. Laws (1876), c. 366.
37 Wis. Laws (1885), c. 247.
38 Wis. Laws (1887), c. 453.
39 Wis. Laws (1871), c. 92.
40 Wis. Laws (1878), c. 212.
41 Wis. Laws (1885), c. 247, § 7.
42 Wis. Laws (1887), c. 453, § 3.
43 Wis. Laws (1911), c. 485.
44 Wis. Laws (1913), c. 599.
45 Wis. Laws (1913), c. 466.

CHAPTER 6

1 O. W. Wight, "Annual Report for 1875," *Geology of Wisconsin,* Vol. II (Madison, Wis., 1877), p. 67.
2 *Ibid.,* p. 68.
3 "Report of Select Committee on the Appointment of a Territorial Geologist," *Journal of the House,* 3 Legis., 1 Sess. (1840), Appendix, p. 146, Doc. P.
4 Wis. Gen. Laws (1853), c. 47.
5 Wis. Rev. Stats. (1849), c. 11, § 9.
6 "Minority Report of the Assembly Judiciary Committee," *Journal of the Assembly,* 7 Legis. (1855), p. 312.
7 Henry Colin Campbell, *Wisconsin in Three Centuries* (New York, 1906), Vol. IV, pp. 198–202.
8 "Annual Report of the Geological Survey," *Journal of the Assembly,* 7 Legis. (1855), Appendix, p. 4.
9 *Journal of the Assembly,* 10 Legis. (1858), pp. 1803, 1809.
10 *Ibid.,* p. 1860.
11 *Journal of the Assembly,* 10 Legis. (1857), pp. 25–26.
12 *Journal of the Assembly,* 10 Legis. (1857), II, Appendix, p. 8; or James B. Percival, "Annual Report of the Geological Survey," *Journal of the Assembly,* 9 Legis. (1856), Appendix, p. 19.
13 Letter quoted in E. F. Bean, "State Geological Surveys of Wisconsin," *Transactions of the Wisconsin Academy of Sciences, Arts and Letters,* Vol. XXX (1937), p. 206.
14 *Journal of the Senate,* 10 Legis. (1858), pp. 181 ff.
15 *Journal of the Senate,* 13 Legis. (1861), p. 1000.
16 *Geology of Wisconsin,* Vol. IV (Madison, Wis., 1882), p. 554; or

J. D. Whitney, *Report of a Survey of the Upper Mississippi Lead Region* (Albany, N.Y., 1862), p. 409.

17 *Journal of the Senate,* 21 Legis. (1869), p. 22.

18 Wis. Gen. Laws (1870), c. 137.

19 *Transactions of the Wisconsin State Agricultural Society* (Madison, Wis., 1870), p. 51.

20 *Journal of the Senate,* 25 Legis. (1872), Appendix, p. 81.

21 *Ibid.,* p. 97.

22 *Journal of the Assembly,* 26 Legis. (1873), Appendix, p. 89.

23 *Ibid.,* p. 118.

24 Wis. Laws (1873), c. 292.

25 One of the assistants, Strong, gave his life in survey service; thrown into the Flambeau River when his boat capsized, he drowned while attempting to rescue a companion who could not swim. Public appreciation of this sacrifice and a favorable public attitude toward the survey caused the legislature to respond to the tragedy by appropriating $1,125 for Strong's widow and children—thus paying him for a full year's work despite the fact that he died after only three months' service.

26 "Annual Report for 1875," reprinted in *Geology of Wisconsin,* Vol. II (Madison, Wis., 1877), p. 71.

27 *Ibid.,* pp. 71–72.

28 Bean, *Transactions of the Wisconsin Academy of Sciences, Arts and Letters,* XXX, 213, n.3.

29 *Ibid.*

30 *American Geologist,* III (1889), 3.

31 *Geology of Wisconsin,* II, 11–12.

32 *Ibid.,* p. 52.

33 *Ibid.,* pp. 57–58.

34 *Ibid.,* p. 751.

35 *Ibid.,* IV, Pt. IV, p. 554.

36 *Ibid.,* Vol. II, p. 372.

37 *Ibid.,* Vol. III, p. 357.

38 Wis. Laws (1876), c. 121, § 1.

39 Wis. Laws (1897), c. 297.

40 Wis. Laws (1903), c. 176.

41 Wis. Laws (1907), c. 641.

42 Wis. Laws (1911), c. 627; Wis. Laws (1949), c. 360.

43 Ulysses S. Grant, *Preliminary Report on the Lead and Zinc Deposits of Southwestern Wisconsin* (Madison, Wis., 1903), p. 88.

44 Ulysses S. Grant, *Report on the Lead and Zinc Deposits of Wisconsin,*

Geological and Natural History Survey Bulletin, No. XIV (Madison, Wis., 1906), pp. 64–65.

45 Ulysses S. Grant, *Preliminary Report on the Copper-Bearing Rocks of Douglas County, Wisconsin,* Geological and Natural History Survey Bulletin, No. VI (2d ed., Madison, Wis., 1901), p. 4.

46 *Ibid.,* p. 53.

47 *Ibid.,* p. 78.

48 *Ibid.,* p. 79.

49 W. O. Hotchkiss, assisted by E. F. Bean and O. W. Wheelwright, *Mineral Land Classification,* Geological and Natural History Survey Bulletin, No. XLIV (Madison, Wis., 1915).

CHAPTER 7

1 *Compania General de Tobacos de Filipinas* v. *Collector of Internal Revenue,* 275 U.S. 87, at p. 100 (1927).

2 Wolfgang Friedman, *Law and Social Change in Contemporary Britain* (London, 1951).

3 Wis. Terr. Stats. (1839), p. 44.

4 Wis. Rev. Stats. (1849), c. 15, § 26.

5 Wis. Gen. Laws (1868), c. 130.

6 Wis. Laws (1877), c. 250.

7 Wis. Laws (1878), c. 334.

8 Wis. Gen. Laws (1868), c. 130, § 16.

9 Anson Marston and Thomas R. Agg, *Engineering Valuation* (New York, 1936), p. 402.

10 See Wis. Laws (1913), c. 672; *Mine Valuation and Assessment,* Geological and Natural History Survey Bulletin, No. XLI (Madison, Wis., 1914).

11 *Ibid.,* pp. 10–11.

12 *Wisconsin State Conservation Commission Report* (1911), p. 3.

13 Letter from Judge Kopp to the author, February 8, 1954.

14 *Ibid.*

15 *State ex rel. Owen* v. *Donald,* 161 Wis. 188, 153 N.W. 238 (1915).

16 Bill 343 S., Wis. Legis. (1955).

17 Wis. Const., Art. XI, § 1.

18 *Milwaukee Sentinel,* February 11, 1954, Part 2, p. 1, col. 1.

CHAPTER 8

1 James Bryce, *The American Commonwealth* (New York, 1888), II, ch. xcvii.

2 Dissenting opinion in *Standard Oil Company* v. *City of Lincoln*, 114 Neb. 243, 255 (1926).
3 *Journal of the Assembly*, 8 Legis. (1856), pp. 613, 639, 670, 813.
4 *Journal of the Assembly*, 10 Legis. (1858), pp. 694, 695, 698, 1542–43.
5 Resolution No. 117 A., *Ibid.*, p. 1159.
6 *Milwaukee Sentinel*, January 18, 1891.
7 Wis. Laws (1907), c. 573.
8 Wis. Laws (1939), c. 456.
9 Wis. Laws (1955), c. 37, § 11.
10 *Journal of the Council*, 2 Legis. Assembly, 1 Sess. (1838), pp. 10 ff.
11 U.S. Stats. at L. (1856, Peters ed.), c. 50, p. 663.
12 *Journal of the Council*, 3 Legis. Assembly, 2 Sess. (1841), p. 26.
13 Wis. Laws (1959), cc. 238, 664.

Index

Accidents. *See* Labor

Adams, John Quincy, 32, 42

Administrative process: in securities regulation, 91, 93, 98, 156, 190; preventive emphasis, 98–99; licensing, 99; in labor regulation, 108–9, 116, 118–22; compared to judicial process, 116; independent status, 193–94

Agriculture, 4, 7, 8, 14, 31, 42, 44, 45, 50, 60, 61, 62, 71, 176

American Mining Company, 127, 129

Antirent Movement, 57

Arnold, Ernest A., promoter, 155, 156

Ashland County, Wisconsin, 12, 145, 157

Ashland Mining Corporation, 171

Assessment of mineral land for taxation. *See* Taxation

Assumption of risk, 103, 104, 106, 116, 191

Aurora Mine, 13

Bank of Mineral Point, 80–81, 83, 181, 189

Banks, 79–81, 82, 83

Baraboo, Wisconsin, 143

Baraboo iron range, 10, 11

Barstow, Governor William A., 127, 128, 129, 130, 131, 132

Bashford, Governor Coles, 133, 134

Bates, Frederick, federal lead-lands supervisor, 22, 23, 26

Bayfield County, Wisconsin, 12

Benton, Senator Thomas Hart, 28–33, 46, 50

Birge, E. A., director, state geological survey, 155

Black River Falls, Wisconsin, 11, 16, 143, 145

Black River Falls Iron Company, 11

Blast furnaces, 16

Board of Health, Wisconsin State, 117, 185

Board of Regents of State Colleges, Wisconsin, 177

Bomford, George, federal lead-lands supervisor, 23, 38, 39

Booms in mining stocks, 13, 14, 91–95, 98. *See also* Depressions; Speculation

Building stone, 152

Bureau of Labor and Industrial Statistics, Wisconsin, 117–18, 120

California, 8, 79, 84

Canal, 7

Capital scarcity: as factor in policy, 78–79, 89, 187; equity and borrowed capital, 88; and tort law, 105, 117; as source of pressure for subsidies, 180. *See also* Factors of Production; Usury Laws

Carr, Ezra, of state geological survey, 133–38 *passim*

Cary Mine, 13

Cazenovia, Wisconsin, 10

Chamberlin, T. C., state geologist, 9, 144, 145, 146, 147, 149, 150, 153

Chicago & Northwestern Railway Company, 4, 10, 12

Child labor, 121, 122